EXPLORING SCIENCE

CARS

AN AMAZING FACT FILE AND HANDS-ON PROJECT BOOK

13 exciting experiments and 280 pictures

PETER HARRISON • CONSULTANT: PETER CAHILL

ARMADILLO

This edition is published by Armadillo,
an imprint of Anness Publishing Ltd; www.armadillobooks.co.uk;
www.annesspublishing.com; Twitter: @Anness_Books

If you like the images in this book and would like to investigate using
them for publishing, promotions or advertising, please visit our website
www.practicalpictures.com for more information.

Publisher: Joanna Lorenz
Editor: Joanne Rippin
Special Photography: John Freeman
Illustrator: Guy Smith
Designer: Sarah Melrose
Production Controller: Stephanie Moe

PUBLISHER'S NOTE
Although the advice and information in this book are believed to be
accurate and true at the time of going to press, neither the authors nor
the publisher can accept any legal responsibility or liability for any
errors or omissions that may have been made nor for any inaccuracies
nor for any loss, harm or injury that comes about from following
instructions or advice in this book.

The publishers would like to thank the following children for appearing
in this book: Amber-Hollie, Emma, Gabrielle, Jamie, Jasmine, Joseph,
Katie, Shaun and Thomas.

PICTURE CREDITS
b=bottom, m=middle, t=top, l=left, r=right
Advertising Archive: 40tl. All Sport: 19tr, 19tl, 19b, 26b,
62b. Agence Vandystadt: 19mr. Alamy: 26ml, 28bl,
29ml, 33br, 38tr, 45br, 49b, 50bl, 57br, 61tl. Art
Archive: 7tr, 36bl. Bridgeman Art Library: 18m. Corbis:
25tl, 25br, 32bl, 34br, 41tr, 43bl, 43br, 49tl, 52b,
53br, 53ml, 55b, 56bl, 60b, 61m, 61b. EON
Productions: 29tl. Genesis: 24bl. Ronald Grant
Archive: 17mr, 29tr, 55t. Getty: 5mr, 14tr, 17tr, 19mr, 21bl, 29b, 43tr,
45tl. Image Bank: 24tl, 34bl. iStock: 1, 5bl, 11tl, 11tr, 33tl, 33ml, 33bl,
36tl, 36br, 38tl, 40m, 50br, 53bl, 57tl, 57tr, 57m, 63br, endpapers. Jaguar:
42tr. LAT: 18bl. Don Morley: 10tr, 10bl, 13tl, 17tl, 22bl, 23tl, 23tr, 23mr,
23br, 24mr, 25tr, 26t, 44tr, 52tl, 53tr, 54b, 59mr, National Motor
Museum: 2b, 3tr, 4br, 28t, 28b, 37mr, 43tl, 49ml, 54t, 54m, 55tr, 61tr.
PA News Photo Library: 28br. Quadrant: 2tl, 4tr, 4bl, 5tr, 5ml, 5tl, 10ml,
11ml, 12br, 13br, 22br, 22tl, 23ml, 23bl, 25bl, 26mr, 30tl, 33tr, 40bl, 41tl,
42br, 44ml, 45ml, 46bl, 48tl, 49mr, 55mr, 56br, 59bl, 63t. Smart Car:
60tl, 60tr. Tony Stone: 3ml, 10tl, 16bl, 25m, 32tl, 36mr, 37tr, 37b, 42bl,
50tl, 56tl, 64bl. Volkswagen Press: 45tr.
Every effort has been made to trace the copyright holders of all images
that appear in this book. Anness Publishing Ltd apologises for any
unintentional omissions and, if notified, would be happy to add an
acknowledgement in future editions.

Manufacturer: Anness Publishing Ltd, 108 Great Russell Street,
London WC1B 3NA, England
For Product Tracking go to: www.annesspublishing.com/tracking
Batch: 7341-23445-1127

CONTENTS

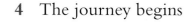

THE JOURNEY BEGINS

Cars make people mobile in a way that would have been impossible a century ago. Then, a journey by road of just 50km/ 30 miles could have taken an entire day. Nowadays, we can travel this distance in half an hour. The ability to go where you want, when you want, quickly, makes getting around much easier. Millions of people all over the world use cars to get to work, to go shopping, to go on holiday or vacation and to visit friends and relations. Horse-drawn carriages and carts, and walking, were the main forms of road transport for thousands of years before cars. Many roads were badly made. Because cars moved under their own power, and encouraged better road building, they allowed people to travel much more.

Hold on tight
Very early cars such as this Velo, made in Germany in 1893 by Karl Benz, had no covering bodywork. When Benz's daughter Clara went driving, she sat high above the road with very little to hang on to if the car hit a bump in the road.

By the numbers
The tachometer (rev. counter), speedometer and clock from a Rolls–Royce Silver Ghost have solid brass fittings and glass covers. They were assembled by hand. The instruments on early cars were often made by skilled craftworkers. The Silver Ghost was made continuously from 1906 until 1925.

Bold as brass
A gleaming brass horn and lamp are proud examples of the detailed work that went into making the first cars. Early cars were made with materials that would be far too expensive for most people nowadays. Seats were upholstered with thickly padded leather, because the cars had poor suspension and bumped a lot. This prevented the drivers and passengers from being jolted up and down too much.

Old bruiser

This Bentley was built before 1931, when the company was taken over by Rolls–Royce. Bentley built powerful and sturdy sports cars, some weighing up to 1,700kg/3,748lb. They won many motor races in the 1920s and 1930s, such as the Le Mans 24-hour race in France. Big cars such as these were built on heavy metal chassis or frames. They had wood–framed bodies covered in metal and leather cloth, huge headlamps and large, wire-spoked wheels.

Egg on wheels

In the 1950s and 1960s, car makers began to make very small cars, such as this German BMW Isetta. Around 160,000 Isettas were produced between 1955 and 1962. Manufacturers developed small cars because they were cheaper to buy and to run, and used less parking space. The Isetta, like so many of the microcars, was powered by a small motorcycle engine.

Cool cruisin'

Cadillac was an American company known for its stylish designs. This Cadillac from the 1950s, with its large tail fins and shiny chrome, is a typical example. Many cars from the 1950s and 1960s, including this one, are known as classic cars. People like to collect them and restore them to their original condition.

Speed and performance

The Italian car maker Ferrari has a reputation for making very fast, very expensive cars. This 2013 F12 Berlinetta has a top speed of 340kmh/210mph. Very few people can afford to own such a car. Even if they have the money, it takes great driving skill to get the best out of one.

Going nowhere?

The success of the car has its downside. Millions of people driving cars causes problems such as traffic jams and air pollution. Also, the building of new roads can spoil the countryside. These issues are being debated all over the world.

THE EARLIEST CARS

Among the most important builders of early cars and car engines were three Germans; Nikolaus Otto, Karl Benz and Gottlieb Daimler. In the late 1800s, they built the first internal combustion engines using sprockets and chains to connect the engine to the wheels. Car engines are called internal combustion (inside burning) engines because they burn a mixture of fuel and air inside a small chamber. People had been trying to make engines for road transport for a long time. In 1770, the Frenchman Nicholas-Joseph Cugnot made a steam engine that drove a three-wheeled cart, but it was too heavy to use and only two were built. The achievement of Benz, Otto and Daimler was to make a small engine that produced enough power for road vehicles. In Britain, the first cars are called veteran (built before 1905) and Edwardian (built between 1905 and 1919). They were not so reliable as modern vehicles, but sometimes better built.

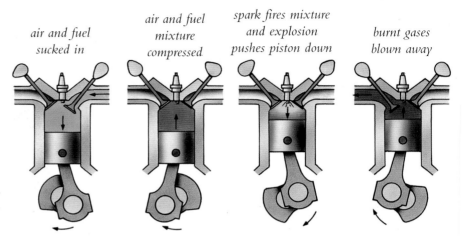

air and fuel sucked in

air and fuel mixture compressed

spark fires mixture and explosion pushes piston down

burnt gases blown away

Suck, squeeze, bang, blow
A car's piston (like an upturned metal cup) moves in a rhythm of four steps called the Otto cycle, after Nikolaus Otto. First, it moves down to suck in fuel mixed with air. Then it pushes up and compresses (squeezes) the mixture. The spark plug ignites the fuel. The bang of the explosion pushes the piston down again. When the piston moves up again, it blows out the burnt gases.

Trim trike
The three-wheeled Benz Motorwagen was first made in 1886. It was steered by a small hand lever on top of a tall steering column. Karl Benz began his career building carriages. He used this training when he built his first car in 1885. By 1888 Benz was employing 50 people to build his Motorwagens.

Follow my leader
Soon after the first cars were being driven on the roads, accidents started to happen. Until 1904, there was a law in Britain requiring a person carrying a red flag to walk in front of the car. This forced the car driver to go slowly. The flag was to warn people that a car was coming.

Remember this

Important military gentlemen pose for photos with their cars. They are not in the driving seats, however. They had chauffeurs to drive the cars for them. Car owners in the early 1900s liked to show their vehicles off. They often posed for photographs to keep for souvenirs.

Look out!

The car horns that early drivers sounded to warn pedestrians were very different from those in modern cars. When the driver squeezed the rubber bulb, air passed through the tube and made a noise when it came out of the end.

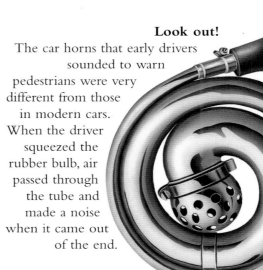

Bad weather

Early cars were hard to control at times because their braking and steering systems were not very effective. When bad weather such as snow made the ground slippery the car could easily run off the road. Even in modern cars with efficient brakes, and good tyres (tires) and steering, winter weather can make driving difficult.

All wrapped up

Drivers at the turn of the century wore thick goggles to protect their eyes, because their cars had no windscreen (windshield) nor any protective bodywork. The roads were not smooth and stones and dust were flung up by the wheels. Cold winds felt even colder in a moving, open car, so thick caps and heavy driving clothes were worn to keep warm.

Nose-to-tail horses

This photograph from the late 1800s shows why we talk about nose-to-tail traffic jams. Before cars were invented, most road transport was by horse-drawn carriage. City streets in those days could become just as jammed with vehicles as they do today.

WHEELS IN MOTION

B EFORE A CAR MOVES, the engine must change the up-and-down movement of the pistons into the round-and-round movement of a shaft (rod) that turns the wheels. With the engine running, the driver presses down the clutch and pushes the gear stick into first gear in the gearbox. The engine turns a shaft called a crankshaft. The power from the turning crankshaft is then transmitted through the gearbox to the wheels on the road. The wheels on the road turn forwards as a result of the combined movement. The wheels turn backwards when the driver pushes the gear stick into reverse gear.

This project shows you how to make a simple machine that creates a similar motion, where one kind of movement that goes around and around can be turned into another kind of movement that goes up and down.

Wind up
The earliest motor cars did not have a starter motor. The driver had to put a starting handle into the front of the car. This connected the handle to the engine's crankshaft to turn it. Turning the handle was hard work and could break the driver's arm if not done correctly. Button-operated starters began to be fitted as early as 1912.

CHANGING MOTION

You will need: shoebox, thin metal rod about 2mm/⅛in diameter, pliers, lid from a jar, masking tape, scissors, thick plastic straw, pencil, piece of stiff paper, at least four different felt-tip pens, thin plastic straw.

1 Place the shoebox narrow-side-down on a flat surface. With one hand push the metal rod through the middle, making sure your other hand will not get jabbed by the rod.

2 Bend the rod at right angles where it comes out of the box. Attach the jar lid to it with adhesive tape. Push the lid until it rests against the side of the box.

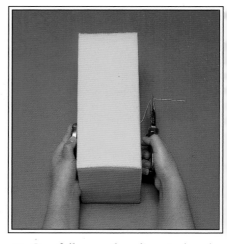

3 Carefully use the pliers to bend the piece of rod sticking out of the other side of the box. This will make a handle for the piston that will be able to turn easily.

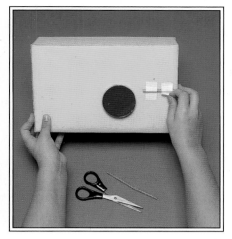

4 Cut a piece of thick plastic straw about 5cm/2in long and tape it to the side of the box close to the jar lid. Make sure that it just sticks up beyond the edge of the box.

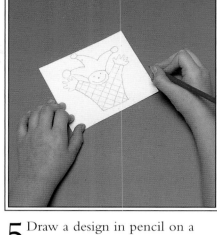

5 Draw a design in pencil on a piece of stiff paper. Copy the jester shown in this project or draw a simple clown. Choose something that looks good when it moves.

6 Using the felt-tip pens, fill in the design until it looks the way you want it to. The brighter the figure is, the nicer it will look on the top of the piston.

7 Carefully cut the finished drawing out of the paper. Make sure you have a clean-edged design. Try not to smudge the felt-tip with your fingers.

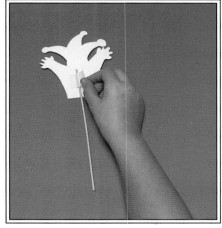

8 Use the masking tape to attach the thin plastic straw to the bottom of the drawing. About 2cm/¾in of straw should be attached.

10 Place the box on end so the jester is at the top. Turn the handle on the left-hand side. As you turn, the jar lid revolves and pushes the jester up and down, like a piston.

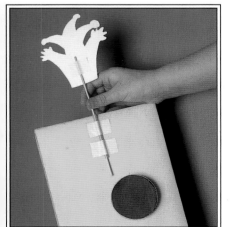

9 Slide the straw attached to the drawing into the straw taped to the back of the box. It will come out of the other end. Push down so that the straw touches the edge of the jar lid.

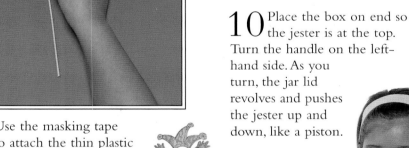

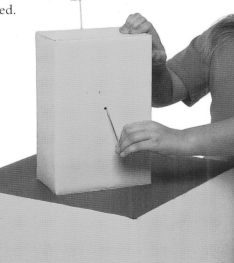

MASS PRODUCTION

Once ways had been found to power a small, wheeled road vehicle, more and more people wanted to own a car. Having one made getting around so much easier. However, early cars were built by hand, piece by piece, which took time. In 1903, the American inventor Henry Ford produced the Model A Ford, the first car designed to be built in large numbers. It gave him the idea to mass-produce all the separate parts of a car in the same place, then have his workers assemble many cars at the same time. This became known as the production-line method. By 1924, 10 million Ford cars had been built. Today, almost all cars are built on production lines and automated machines do much of the work. Some cars are still built by hand, but they can be built only very slowly. For example, the British car maker Morgan makes an average of 25 cars a week, while the Ford motor company can build between 8,000 and 10,000 per day across their 200 factories.

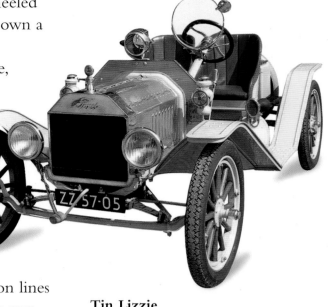

Tin Lizzie
The Model T Ford was the world's first mass-produced (assembled on a production line) car. Millions were made and sold all over the world. Nowadays people collect examples of these cars, which were called Tin Lizzies, maintaining, restoring and repairing them, often to a gleaming state. It is unlikely that they would have been so well cared for by their original owners.

Herbert's big idea
The Austin Seven was one of the most popular cars ever. This version is a sporting two seater. Between 1922 and 1938 there were many versions, including racing cars and even vans. The Austin Motor Company was founded by Herbert Austin in 1903. The company allowed other car makers to build the Austin Seven in France, Japan, America and Germany.

Beetling around
In 1937, the German government founded a car company to build cheap cars. The car, designed by Dr Ferdinand Porsche, was called the Volkswagen, meaning "people's car", but it gained the nickname of the "Beetle" because of its unusual shape. Some people painted their Beetles for fun. By the 1960s, the car was popular worldwide. By 2000, over 21 million Volkswagons had been sold.

Next one, please

Modern cars are made with the help of machines in factories. Each machine does a different job. Some weld metal parts together, others attach fittings and secure fastenings, others spray paint. The car's metal body parts come together on a moving track that runs past each machine. Making cars like this means they can be put together quickly and in vast numbers.

Big yellow taxi

For people without a car, such as tourists, taxis are a convenient way of getting around in towns and cities. Taxi drivers try to find the best short cuts for an easy journey. Hiring a taxicab also means that people don't have to find a place to park. The bright yellow "checker cabs" in New York became a symbol for the city all over the world. Some of the classic models are still in use today.

The people's servant

The Trabant was from East Germany. Many millions were built for ordinary people. Its name comes from a Hungarian word meaning "servant", and the Trabant served as a cheap, reliable car across Eastern Europe. This 601 model was first made in 1964.

Alec's big idea

Launched in 1959, the Morris Mini Minor was one of the most revolutionary cars of the last 50 years. It was cheap to buy and cheap to run, easy to drive and easy to park. Despite its small size, it could carry four people comfortably. The car's designer, Alec Issigonis, a British citizen of Greek parentage, also designed the Morris Minor, a small family car launched in 1948.

THE ENGINE

A CAR'S ENGINE is made up of metal parts, which are designed to work together smoothly and efficiently. In older cars, a valve called a carburettor feeds a mixture of air and fuel into the cylinder, where the mixture is burnt to produce power. Newer cars often use an injection system, which measures and controls the amount of fuel into the engine more accurately. To keep the engine cool, water is pumped from the radiator and circulated around chambers in the cylinder block. The waste gases created by the burnt fuel are carried away by the exhaust system. The engine sucks in the air and petrol (gasoline) mixture and allows it to burn. To help the moving parts move against each other smoothly, they are lubricated with oil from the engine oil sump. A pump squirts the oil on to the parts.

A car's electrical power is driven by an alternator. The electrical current is stored in the battery. This provides the electricity to start the engine and for the power steering, lights, heater and air conditioning, electric windows, sound system and computer.

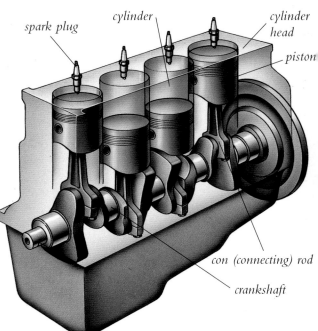

spark plug — cylinder — cylinder head — piston — con (connecting) rod — crankshaft

Working together
Most car engines have four cylinders. In each cylinder a piston moves up and down. Four rods, one from each piston, turn metal joints attached to the crankshaft. As the rods turn the joints, the crankshaft moves around and around. The movement is transmitted to the wheels, using the gearbox to control how fast the wheels turn relative to the engine.

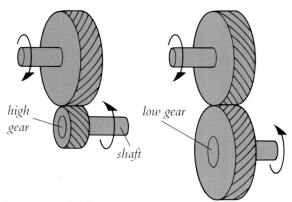

high gear — shaft — low gear

Wheels within wheels
The car's engine turns a shaft or rod with different sized gears (toothed wheels) on it. High gears are used for more speed because when a big wheel turns a small one, it turns faster. The gear system is called the transmission, because it transmits or moves the engine's power to the wheels. Cars have five or six forward gears. The biggest is for slow speeds, and the smallest for high speeds. When the car goes around corners, its wheels move at different speeds.

Turbo tornado
This 1997 Dodge engine can make a car go especially fast because it has a turbocharger that forces the fuel and air mixture faster and more efficiently into the engine cylinder head. Turbochargers are driven by waste exhaust gases drawn away from the exhaust system, which is a way of turning the waste gases to good use. Turbochargers are very effective at boosting engine power.

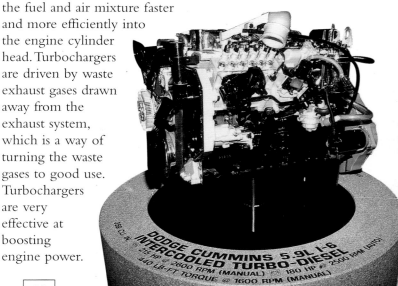

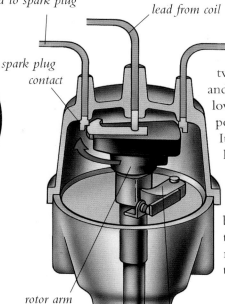

Power control
The distributor has two jobs. It connects and disconnects low-value electric power to the coil. It also supplies high-value electric power from the coil to each spark plug. This makes a spark big enough to ignite the air and fuel mixture at exactly the right time.

lead to spark plug

lead from coil

spark plug contact

rotor arm

contact breaker

What you see is what you get
This vintage racing Bentley displays its twin carburettors mounted on a supercharger (a mechanically driven device similar to a turbocharger) in front of the engine. The water pipes from the radiator to the engine, electric leads, plug leads and large open exhaust pipes can all be seen.

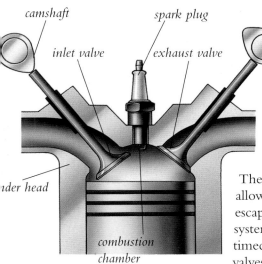

camshaft

spark plug

inlet valve

exhaust valve

cylinder head

combustion chamber

Double movement
The camshaft opens and closes the inlet and exhaust valves. The valves are fitted into the cylinder head, and open and close holes in the combustion chamber. The exhaust valve opens to allow burnt waste gases to escape into the car's exhaust system. The spark plug is timed to spark when both valves have closed both holes.

See and be seen
The lights used on early cars usually burned either oil or gas. Oil was carried in a small container in the bottom of the lamp. Gas was created by dissolving in water tablets of carbide (carbon mixed with metal) carried in a canister.

Blow them away
Mercedes–Benz fitted a supercharger to this 1936 540K to add power to the engine. The German company first used superchargers on their racing cars in 1927. This method of adding power had first been used on aircraft engines in 1915.

IN THE RIGHT GEAR

GEARS ARE toothed wheels that interlock with each other to transfer movement. They have been used in machines of many kinds for over 2,000 years. In a car gearbox, the gears are arranged on shafts so that they interlock when the driver changes from one gear to the next. Cars have five or six forward gears depending on the design, use and cost of the car. Several gears are needed because driving requires different combinations of speed and force at different times.

The largest gear wheel is bottom gear. It turns slower than the higher gears. It provides more force and less speed for when the car is moving from stop, or going uphill. In top gear, less force and more speed is provided. The top gear wheel is the smallest and rotates the fastest. This project connects two gears to show the beautiful patterns that gears can make. Then you can make your own three-gear machine.

Uphill struggle
Pushing a car up a steep hill in a 1920s car rally put a lot of strain on the low gears in a car. On steep slopes, first and second gears are often the only ones that a driver can use. Fourth gear is for the flat, and fifth and sixth gears are for cruising at high speeds.

DRAWING WITH GEARS

You will need: pair of compasses (compass), A4/8½x11in sheet of white paper, black pen, scissors, A4/8½x11in sheet of card (card stock), two strips of corrugated cardboard, adhesive tape, three different felt-tip pens.

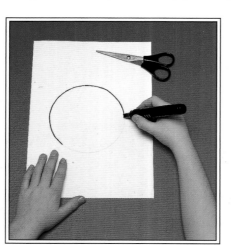

1 Using the compasses, trace a 14cm/5½in diameter circle on the paper. Draw over it with the pen and cut it out. On the card, trace, draw and cut out a circle with a diameter of 11cm/4½in.

2 Tape corrugated cardboard around the circles. Make a hole in the small circle wide enough for the tip of a felt-tip pen. Turn the small wheel inside the larger. Trace the path in felt-tip pen.

3 Make a second hole in the small wheel. Turn the small gear inside the larger using another felt-tip pen. Make a third hole in the small wheel and use the third pen to create an exciting, geometric design.

3-GEAR MACHINE

You will need: *pair of compasses (compass), A4/8½x11in sheet of cardboard, pen, scissors, three strips of corrugated cardboard, adhesive tape, A4/8½x11in piece of fibreboard, glue, 6cm/2½in piece of 12mm/½in diameter wood dowel, three map (push) pins.*

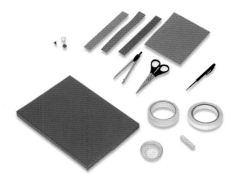

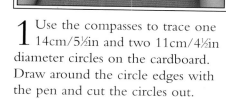

1 Use the compasses to trace one 14cm/5½in and two 11cm/4½in diameter circles on the cardboard. Draw around the circle edges with the pen and cut the circles out.

2 Carefully wrap the strips of corrugated cardboard around the circles, using one strip per circle, corrugated side out. Tape each strip to the bottom of the circles.

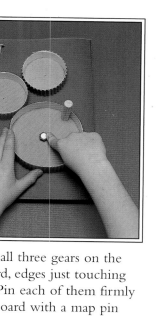

3 Place the largest gear wheel on the piece of fibreboard. Hold the gear down and glue the dowel on to the side of the gear base at the edge of the wheel. Leave it until it is dry.

4 Position all three gears on the fibreboard, edges just touching each other. Pin each of them firmly to the fibreboard with a map pin but allow them to turn.

6 Now you have a three-gear machine where the energy from each gear is being transferred to the other, just like the gears in a car.

5 Gently turn the dowel on the largest gear. As that gear turns, the two others that are linked together by the corrugated cardboard will turn against it. See how they move in opposite directions to each other.

SAFE RIDE AND HANDLING

MOST MODERN cars have four wheels. The wheels tend to be placed one at each corner, which helps to distribute the car's weight evenly on the road. An evenly balanced car rides and handles well and has good road grip and braking. Engine power usually drives either the front or rear wheels, but for cars that are designed for off-road driving for pleasure, all-wheel drive is becoming more popular. Driving safely at speed in a straight line or around corners is a test of how well a car has been designed. Modern cars have power-assisted steering to make steering easier. Tyres (tires) are an important part of good road handling. The tread pattern and grooves are designed to make the tyre grip the road efficiently, especially in wet, slippery conditions.

Big bopper

The French tyre manufacturer Michelin has been making tyres since 1888. The Michelin brand has been known for many years by the sign of a human figure that looks as though it is made out of tyres.

Gripping stuff

Tyre tread patterns have raised pads, small grooves and water-draining channels to grip the road surface. There are different kinds of tyres for cars, buses, trucks and tractors. Tyre makers also make tyres for different road conditions. Examples include winter tyres and special run-flat tyres that stay hard even when they are damaged.

Dig deep

Tractor tyres are very deeply grooved. This allows them to grip hard in slippery mud. The width of the tyres spreads the weight of the heavy vehicle over soft ground. The tyres are high so that the tractor can ride easily over obstacles on the ground, such as big rocks.

Burn the rubber

Racing car tyres are wide so that the car can go as fast as possible while maintaining grip and stability on the road. They are made in very hard mixtures of rubber to cope with varying amounts of heat generated by racing in different conditions. Ordinary tyres would melt.

Out for a spin

Until very light alloy wheels became available in the last 30 years, sports cars had wire-spoke wheels. These combined strength with lightness, both important features in a sports car. When a sports car brakes or turns sharply, modern alloy wheels are strong enough to take the strain. Alloy wheels can also be fitted to ordinary cars.

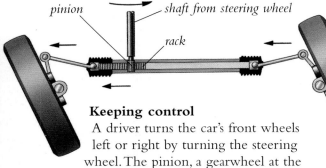

pinion *shaft from steering wheel* *rack*

Keeping control

A driver turns the car's front wheels left or right by turning the steering wheel. The pinion, a gearwheel at the bottom of the steering shaft, interlocks with a toothed rack. This is connected to the wheels via a system of joints and wheels. As the steering wheel turns, the movement of the pinion along the rack turns the road wheels.

King of the castle

Very large trucks that carry heavy loads use enormous tyres to spread the weight. This flatbed truck has been fitted with earthmover tyres for fun. Look how much bigger they are than the ones on the car this truck is rolling over.

Firm in the wet

Driving at speed on a wet road can be dangerous. Water can form a film that is able to lift a tyre clear of the road for several seconds. To prevent this, tyre makers mould drain channels into the tread to push the water away from under the tyre as it rotates.

SPEED CONTESTS

RACING CARS against one another to test their speed and endurance has gone on for over 120 years. The American car maker Henry Ford, for example, designed and built racing cars before he set up the Ford car factory in 1903. Many kinds of car race now take place, including stock car, rally, speedway and drag racing. The FIA (*Fédération Internationale de l'Automobile*) makes rules about issues such as the tracks, the design and power of the cars, and the safety of drivers and spectators.

The fastest and most powerful kind of track racing is Formula One, also known as Grand Prix racing. The cars can travel up to 380kmh/240mph on straight sections of track. As the races are so exciting, the best drivers are paid in the millions. Formula One winners, such as Lewis Hamilton and Sebastian Vettel, are international celebrities. Technological advances in production-line cars have often been developed and tested in Grand Prix cars.

GRAND-PRIX Dieppe de l'A·C·F· 1907 NAZZARO su F·I·A·T·

Your move

When racing drivers complete a race and cross the finishing line, a race official waves a black and white flag known as the chequered flag. The black and white pattern of squares on the finishing flag looks like the pattern on a chessboard. It is known all over the world as the sign of motor racing.

Monster motors

Early Grand Prix cars, such as this 10.2 litre Fiat, had enormous engines. Grand Prix racing began in France in 1904 and slowly spread to other countries. The *Association Internationale des Automobiles Clubs Reconnus* (AIACR) set the rules for races until it was reformed as the FIA in 1946.

Furious Ferrari

The Italian car maker Ferrari has been making racing cars since 1940. Here Michael Schumacher, driving the Ferrari F399, rounds a curve on the 4.7km/7½-mile Catalunya circuit at the 1999 Barcelona Grand Prix.

FACT BOX

• Between 1992 and 2012, the German driver Michael Schumacher won a total of 91 Formula One races, the highest number so far achieved by any driver.

• Ayrton Senna won the Monaco Grand Prix a record six times between 1987 and 1993.

• Until 1961, the track at Indianapolis, USA, was known as "the brickyard" because it was partly paved with bricks.

Take-off

The speeds at which rally cars travel mean they often fly over the tops of the hills on the course. The driver and navigator of this car in the 1999 Portuguese Rally are strapped in to their seats to protect them from the tremendous thump that will come when the car's four wheels touch the ground in a second or two.

Take it to the limit

The heat generated by this Top Fuel drag racer's engine at the 1996 NHRA (*National Hot Rod Association*) Winternational makes the air vibrate around it. Drag races are short, like sprint races for athletes. The races take place over a straight course only 402m/440 yards long, and the cars can reach speeds of 530kmh/330mph. The flat spoilers on the front and rear of the cars are pushed down by the air rushing past, helping to keep the car on the road.

The chase

Tight bends are a test of driving skills for Formula One drivers. The cars brake hard from very high speeds as they approach the bend. Drivers try not to leave any gap that following cars could use for overtaking. As the drivers come out of the bend they accelerate as hard as is possible without skidding and going into a spin.

Making a splash

Rally car driving is extremely tough on the cars and on the drivers. Cars drive over deserts, mud-filled roads, rivers, snow and many other obstacles. The cars follow the same route, but start at different times. The course is divided into separate sections known as Special Stages. There is a time limit for each stage. The winner of the rally is the car that has the fastest overall time.

Thrill becomes spill

The Brazilian Mauricio Gugelmin's car soars into the air at the 1985 French Grand Prix, crashing to the ground upside down. The driver survived and has since taken part in many Grand Prix races. Safety regulations have greatly improved since then.

RACE TRACKS

PEOPLE HAVE been racing cars on specially designed public circuits (tracks) almost since cars were invented. The first race on a special circuit took place in 1894 in France. The Italian track at Monza is one of the oldest racing circuits. It was built for the 1922 Italian Grand Prix. Among the best-known tracks are Silverstone and Brands Hatch in Great Britain, Indianapolis in the USA, the Nurbürgring in Germany, and Monaco. Millions of people all over the world watch the races at these tracks and on television. The teams and the drivers compete furiously with one another to prove whose car is the fastest. Very rarely the competition can be so fierce it is deadly. Ayrton Senna died at Imola in Italy in 1994, and Jules Bianchi was killed in a crash in Japan in 2014. In this project, you can build your own race track, specially designed to let your cars build up speed on a steep slope, and race against a partner to see whose car is the fastest.

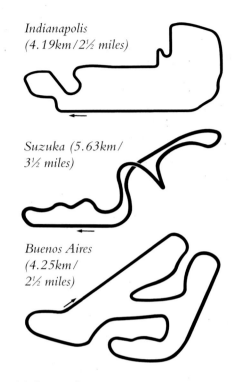

Indianapolis (4.19km/2½ miles)

Suzuka (5.63km/ 3½ miles)

Buenos Aires (4.25km/ 2½ miles)

TESTING GROUND

You will need: 25cm/10in of 8cm/3in diameter card tube, scissors, small paintbrush, blue paint, ten strips of paper 6x2cm/2½x¾in, masking tape, two strips of white paper 1.5x8cm/½x3in, pencil, red and black felt-tip pens, pieces of paper in white and other shades, cocktail sticks (toothpicks), A4/8½x11in sheet of red card (card stock), ruler, two small model cars.

Twist and turn
All racetracks, such as those shown above, test the skill of the drivers and the speed and handling of the racing cars. They combine bends with straight stretches. Sharp bends are known as hairpin bends. Most tracks are 4–5.5km/2½–3½ miles in length.

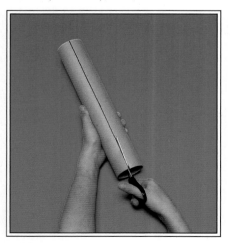

1 Use the scissors carefully to cut the cardboard tube in half along its length. Hold the tube in one hand but make sure you keep the scissor blades away from your hands.

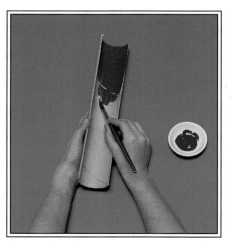

2 Use the paintbrush to apply a thick coat of blue paint to the inside of both halves of the tube. To give a strong blue, paint a second coat after the first has dried.

3 Use masking tape to stick the ten narrow strips of paper together. Tape them along their widths to make a flexible bend. This joins the racetrack together.

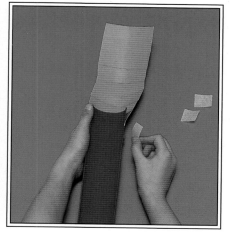

4 Now take the flexible bend you have made from strips of paper. Tape it to one end of one of the painted halves of the tube. Use small pieces of masking tape.

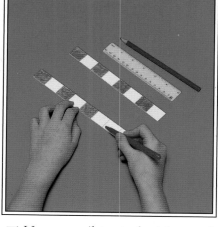

5 Use a pencil to mark eight equal 1cm/½in blocks on both strips of white paper. Draw in alternate red blocks with a felt-tip pen to make striped crash barriers.

6 Draw 1cm/⅛in black and white squares on to a 4x8cm/1½x3in piece of paper. Cut the other paper pieces into pennants (forked flags). Tape the flags to cocktail sticks.

7 Cut three 8cm/3in wide strips from the sheet of red card. Use scissors to cut a semicircle out of the top of each of the strips.

8 Measure with a ruler and cut the three strips to varying heights of 20cm/8in, 14cm/5½in and 7cm/2¾in. Tape them to the underside of half of the tube, fitting them on at the semicircle shapes to support the half tube in a gradual slope.

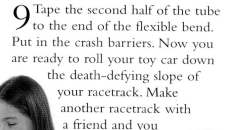

9 Tape the second half of the tube to the end of the flexible bend. Put in the crash barriers. Now you are ready to roll your toy car down the death-defying slope of your racetrack. Make another racetrack with a friend and you can race each other's cars.

Popping the cork
Lewis Hamilton sprays his race-winning teammate Nico Rosberg with champagne during the Austrian Formula One Grand Prix in June 2015 in Spielberg, Austria.

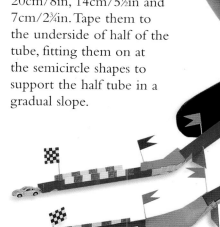

COLLECTING

THE CARS that were made many years ago have not been forgotten. In Britain, they are known as veteran (made before 1905), Edwardian (1905–19), vintage (1919–30) and Classics. Enthusiasts (people with a special interest) all over the world collect and maintain old cars. They value them for many reasons, such as the great care that went into making them, their design, their engine power and their rarity. Clubs such as the AACA (Antique Automobile Club of America) and FIVA (*Fédération Internationale Véhicules Anciens*) exist for the collectors of old American and European cars. There are also specific clubs for owners of particular models of car. Owners like to meet up and compare notes on maintaining their vehicles. Their clubs organize tours and rallies in which owners can drive their cars in working order.

Annual get-together
Veteran cars (built before 1905) parade along the sea front in Brighton, England. The London-to-Brighton veteran car run has been held every year (except during wartime) since 1904. It celebrates cars being driven without someone with a red flag walking in front to warn of their approach.

Who stole the roof?
Early vehicles were built on the frames of horse-drawn wagons, so they had little protective bodywork. Drivers and their passengers had to wrap up well when driving.

Room for two?
Frenchman Louis Delage built cars with great engineering skill. The engine of this 1911 racing model was so big that there was little room for the driver. The huge tube in the bonnet (hood) carried exhaust gases to the back of the car.

High roller
The Rolls–Royce Silver Ghost is one of the great early vintage cars. It was first built in 1906. Almost 8,000 were made before production finally stopped in 1925. By that time, fewer people were able to afford such large, expensive cars. Individual buyers could have the car's specification and equipment altered according to their own needs. Several Silver Ghosts were produced as armoured cars to protect top British Army generals during World War I.

Mighty midget
The 1930 MG Midget was a powerful small car and clearly deserved its name. The Midget was the first car that the MG company sold in large numbers. Its success allowed the firm to expand and become more widely known.

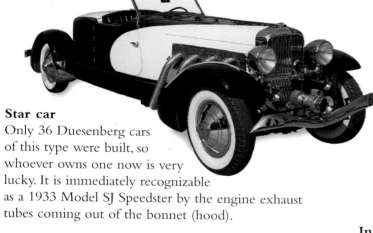

Star car
Only 36 Duesenberg cars of this type were built, so whoever owns one now is very lucky. It is immediately recognizable as a 1933 Model SJ Speedster by the engine exhaust tubes coming out of the bonnet (hood).

Mint condition
The owners of old cars have to give a great deal of loving care to the car's engine. Keeping an original MG Midget engine running demands patience in finding spare parts, maintaining old metal and making regular tests.

Starry Ferrari
The Italian company Ferrari is one of the world's greatest car makers. Owning a Ferrari has always been seen as a symbol of wealth and success, so the cars are favourites with film stars and sports stars. This 166 Ferrari is from the late 1940s.

In demand
This 1930s racing car combines style and power, qualities that still give Alfa Romeo its strong reputation. Collectors today value racing cars of the past just as much as passenger cars. The Italian car maker Alfa Romeo has been building fast cars since 1915.

OFF-ROAD VEHICLES

Seaside fun
Driving on beaches is difficult because wheels can sink into the wet sand. Vehicles for driving on a beach are built to be very light, with balloon tyres to spread the vehicle's weight over a wide area.

Most cars are designed for driving on smooth roads. There are specialized vehicles, however, that can drive across rough terrain such as mud, desert and stony ground. Off-road vehicles are usually called SUVs (sport utility vehicles) and cars of this kind often have four-wheel drive, large tyres (tires) and very tough suspension. They stand high off the ground and have strong bodywork. The earliest off-road vehicles were the US Jeep and the British Land Rover. The Jeep, made by Ford and Willys, started life in World War II. It was designed to travel across roads damaged by warfare. The Land Rover, built by the Rover company in the late 1940s, was based on the idea of the Jeep. It was intended for farmers, who have to drive across difficult terrain. The Land Rover proved useful in all parts of the world where roads were poor or non-existent. Driving off-road is still a necessity in many places. In recent times, it has also become a leisure activity for drivers who like to test their driving skills in difficult places.

Tough cookie
At the start of World War II the United States Army developed a vehicle with a sturdy engine, body and chassis. The wheels were at the corners for stability over rough ground. The GP (General Purpose) vehicle became known as the Jeep.

No traffic jams
The Lunar Rover, carried to the Moon by *Apollo 17* in 1971, was powered by electricity. The low gravity of the moon meant that it would not sink into soft ground. A wide track and long wheelbase stopped it from turning over if it hit a rock.

Angel of mercy

This outreach vehicle from the Bwindi Community Hospital on the edge of an impenetrable forest in Western Uganda helps doctors take medical aid to people living in remote areas where there are few roads. A four-wheel drive car is able to cross shallow rivers and rough terrain.

Hospital on wheels

Aid agencies such as UNICEF and *Mèdecins Sans Frontières* use specially adapted trucks fitted out as mobile hospitals. They help to save lives in times of war and natural disaster. Heavily reinforced bodywork protects patients and easily damaged medical supplies.

Electric caddies

A typical game of golf involves covering 5km/3 miles or more. Golfers need an easy way to carry heavy golf clubs around the course. Golf karts, also called golf buggies, are simple, light vehicles powered by electricity. They have enough battery life to carry golfers and their clubs from the first to the last hole on the course.

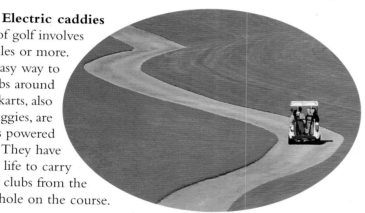

FACT BOX
• The Dakar Rally is one of the world's best-known off-road races. Founded in 1978 by the French driver Thierry Sabine and originally running from Paris to Dakar, it has been held in South America since 2009 and has up to 400 vehicles competing each year.

Get tracking

Half-tracks played an important part in World War II, and still do in modern warfare. They have tracks at the rear to allow them to travel over very broken surfaces. The wheels at the front give added mobility that tanks do not have.

Dune bashing

In the Arabian Desert four-wheel drive cars such as Toyota Landcruisers are used to take tourists on an exciting drive over sand dunes. It's been described as a roller coaster on the ground; you have to fasten your seatbelts very tightly.

CUSTOM-BUILT

SOMETIMES SERIOUS car enthusiasts decide to adapt a standard model. They might alter the engine to make it run faster, or change the body to make it look different. Cars specially adapted like this are known as custom cars. Custom cars have become very popular since the 1950s, particularly in the USA. The wheels may be taken from one kind of car, the body from a second, the mudguards and engine from others, and the different parts are combined to make a completely original car. The end result can be dramatic. These unusual cars have many different names, such as mean machines, street machines, muscle machines and hot rods. Racing custom cars is a popular activity. Stock cars are custom cars built especially for races in which crashes often occur. Drag racers are incredibly fast and powerful cars built for high speed races over short distances.

Water baby
Surf's up and this muscle machine is on the tideline. This cool dude has fitted big, wide tyres (tires) on a roadster body to spread the car's weight on soft sand. He has also been busy with a paintbrush, adding flames to the body.

Made to measure
This car is a mixture of styles. The driver's cab and steering wheel have been made to look like those in a veteran car. The modern engine is chrome-plated, with all the parts visible. The exhaust-outlet tubes resemble those from a 1930s racing car. The front wheels are bigger than the rear ones.

Soft furnishings
Some people change the insides of their cars to create a truly luxurious look. They replace the standard fittings, for example, with soft leather seats, padded dashboards and leather-covered gear shifts.

Really smokin'
The grille on the bonnet (hood) of this customized hot rod is the turbocharger. It can boost the engine to speeds of 400kmh/250mph. When the car brakes at high speed, its tyres make lots of smoke because they are burning from friction with the road.

FLUFFY DICE

You will need: *box at least 12cm/4½in square, two A4/8½x11in sheets of white paper, masking tape, scissors, 20cm/8in string, 80cm/31in square of furry fabric, pencil, bradawl (awl), glue, circle stencil.*

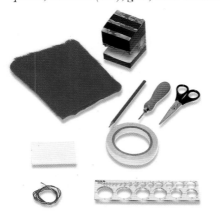

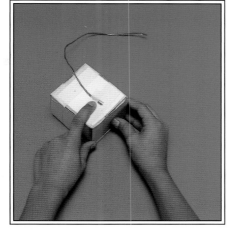

1 Stick white paper around all six surfaces of the box with tape. Use a piece of masking tape to stick 3cm/1¼in of the end of the length of string to one side of the box.

2 Place the fabric furry-side down. Put the box at one edge and draw around it. Then roll the box over and draw around it again. Do six squares like this to form a cross.

3 Cut out the cross shape. With a bradawl, carefully make a hole in the middle of the central square. Place the box face down on the fur and pull the string through the hole.

4 Spread glue evenly on the inside of each square of the fabric, one at a time. Press the glued material squares on to the box faces.

5 Choose a medium-size circle shape from the circle stencil. Using a pencil, draw 21 of the same circles on to the piece of white paper.

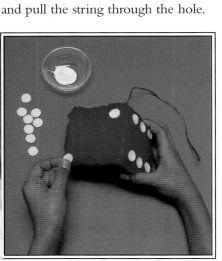

6 Cut out the circles. Glue them on to the furry side of the fabric. Put six dots on one face, five dots on the next, then four, three, two and finally one dot. You could use a real dice to see the correct arrangement.

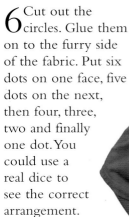

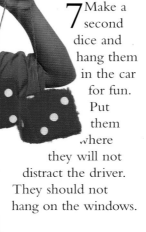

7 Make a second dice and hang them in the car for fun. Put them where they will not distract the driver. They should not hang on the windows.

UNUSUAL DESIGNS

CARS ARE often adapted (have their design changed) to suit different needs, or just for fun. Three-wheeled cars, a kind of microcar, are cheap to run and take up less road space than the conventional four-wheeled cars.

Amphibious vehicles that can operate on land and water were built in World War II for fighting. Since then, specialist German, British and Chinese manufacturers have gone on building small numbers of these cars for use in regions with many rivers.

Films studios often create sensational special effects around cars that appear to have special powers. Then there are the real but wacky cars, made by people who want to create cars that defy the imagination. These have included cars that split down the middle, cars that are covered in fur, and cars that look like sofas or cans of baked beans.

Frog face
The microcars produced in in the 1950s and 1960s were for driving in towns. This 1959 Messerschmitt had a tiny engine and was just 2.7m/9ft long. Even so, it had a top speed of 100kmh/65mph. The top of the car swings over to allow the driver entry. The car was also very cheap to run. It used only one litre of petrol every 24km/60 miles, almost half the fuel consumption of a modern car.

Bedtime car
This car may look like a double bed, but in order to travel on a public highway it needs to conform to all the regulations of the road. It will have passed an annual inspection for safety and road worthiness. Headlights, a registration plate and seat belts are fitted.

Supermarket beep
A giant supermarket trolley (cart) has been constructed and fitted with a car engine. This vehicle is strictly for fun. Lacking basic safety features such as proper seats, lights and bumpers, it is not allowed to be driven on public roads.

Only in the movies
The 1977 James Bond film, *The Spy Who Loved Me*, featured a car that behaved as though it was also a submarine. It was a British Lotus Elite car body specially altered to create the illusion.

Magic car
Ian Fleming, the creator of James Bond, also wrote a book about a magic car. This became the 1968 film *Chitty Chitty Bang Bang*. The car was an old one that the book's hero, Caractacus Potts, discovered in a junkyard. After restoring it, he discovered it could fly and float.

Juice car
This Fiat car has been adapted to sell juices and shakes, complete with a counter, equipment and lots of fruit.

Replica style
This 3-wheeler Triking, a modern replica (copy) of a 1930s Morgan, is a kit car that has been put together. The owner is supplied with all the different body panels and engine parts, and builds the complete car. Kit cars are cheaper than production-line cars, because the costs of assembly and labour are saved.

Web-toed drivers
Cars that can cross water are useful, and fun. Between 1961 and 1968, the German Amphicar company made almost 4,000 amphibious cars. In 2004 Richard Branson drove a Gibbs Aquada across the English Channel in just 1 hour, 40 minutes and 6 seconds. The car, which is no longer in production, reaches speeds of 160kmh/99mph on land and 50kmh/31mph at sea.

COOLING SYSTEM

THE EXPLOSIONS in a car's engine, and the friction caused by its moving parts, create a great deal of heat. If the heat was not kept down, the engine would stop working. The metal parts would expand, seize up and stop. To cool the engine, water from a radiator is pumped through chambers in the cylinder block. The moving water carries heat away from the hottest parts of the engine. The radiator has to be cooled down too. A fan blows air on to it, to cool the water inside. The fan is driven by a belt from the engine crankshaft pulley. This project shows you how to transfer the energy of turning motion from one place to another. It uses a belt to move five reels.

FAN BELT

Rear engine

The air-cooled rear-engined Volkswagen Beetle was designed with an aerodynamic front and no need for a front-mounted radiator. Instead, the engine is cooled by a fan driven by a fan belt, like the one shown here. Engines of this kind are useful in cold climates, where low temperatures can freeze water in radiators.

You will need: *ruler, 16cm/6¼in square of thin cloth, scissors, five cotton reels (bobbins), A4/8½x 11in wooden board, glue stick, pencil, five flat-headed nails 4cm1½in in length, hammer, 1m/39in length of 2.5cm/1in wide velvet ribbon, adhesive tape, pair of compasses (compass), five pieces of 15cm/6in square card (card stock) in different shades, five wooden skewers.*

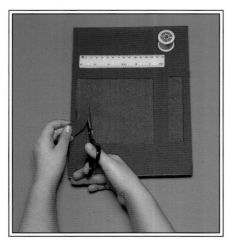

1 Measure five 2.5cm/1in wide strips on the thin cloth. The height of the cotton reels should be more than 2.5cm/1in. Use the scissors to cut out each strip.

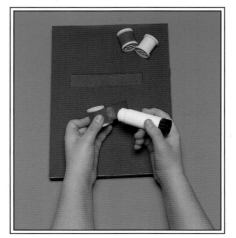

2 Wrap one of the fabric strips around each of the five cotton reels. Glue each strip at the end so that it sits firmly around the reel and does not come loose.

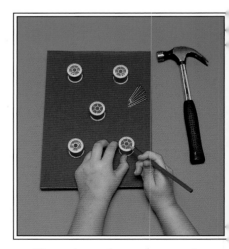

3 Place the reels on the wooden board as shown above. Trace the outlines with a pencil. Put the nails through the middle of the reels and hammer them into the board.

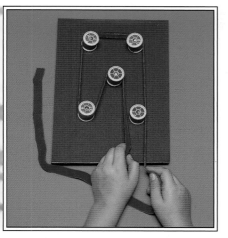

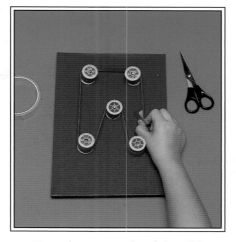

4 Wind the ribbon around the reels with the velvet side against four of the reels. Cut the ribbon at the point where you can join both ends around the fifth reel.

5 Tape the two ends of the ribbon together firmly. Make sure that the ribbon wraps firmly around all of the five reels, but not so tightly that it cannot move.

6 Use the pair of compasses to draw circles about 7cm/2¾in in diameter on to the card squares. Then draw freehand spiral shapes inside each circle.

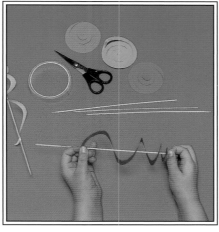

10 Now you are ready to turn the belt. Like a fan belt in a car, it turns the fans around. This is a five-fan machine. You can add more fans if you like.

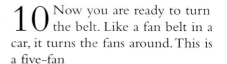

7 Use scissors to cut each spiral out of each of the card squares. Start from the outside edge and gradually work your way in along the lines of the spiral.

8 Tape one end of the spiral to the end of a skewer. Wind the other end of the spiral around the skewer stick a few times. Tape it close to the opposite end of the skewer.

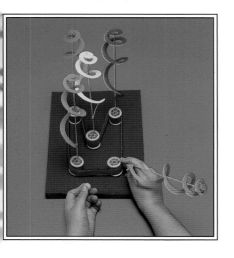

9 Put a small amount of adhesive tape on the end of each skewer. Then place each skewer into one of the empty holes in the top of each cotton reel.

ENVIRONMENT MATTERS

CARS ARE convenient, but their effect on the environment causes great concern. The manufacture, and driving of cars both use up precious natural resources such as metals, water and oil. The emissions (waste gases) that petrol cars produce also pollute the atmosphere. One of them, carbon monoxide, is thought by many scientists to be contributing to problems such as global warming (the warming of the world's climate because of gases trapped in the atmosphere).

Although the environmental problems associated with cars are severe, car makers have made many improvements to their models during recent years. Cars are much lighter than they used to be, so smaller amounts of raw materials are needed to make them. Because they are lighter and their engines are more efficient, they can drive further for each litre of fuel than previously. In many countries, the emission of carbon monoxide into the atmosphere is actually lower now than thirty years ago, despite there being many more cars.

Costly accident

The petrol (gasoline) that cars burn is extracted from oil pumped out of the ground or from under the sea. The oil is transported in enormous ships to refineries where the petrol is extracted. Occasionally, a tanker sinks or is holed. When this happens, oil seeps into the sea and forms a slick on the surface, killing and injuring fish and birds.

FACT BOX
• Ford launched the Ford Fiesta in 1976, and the Ford Ka in 1998. Both were small everyday cars. But the exhaust gases of the 1976 Ford Fiesta contained 50 times more pollutants, such as carbon monoxide and nitrogen oxides, than the 1998 Ford Ka.

Plug-in car

Electric cars are better for the environment than petrol or diesel cars and have become much more efficient and affordable. In most European countries, like here in Paris, there are also now better public recharging networks, so that you can plug your car in on the street and in car parks.

Giving pedestrians space

There are too many cars in the world. Traffic congestion in towns and cities is a serious problem in many countries. City park-and-ride schemes allow drivers to park outside a town, then catch a free bus to the middle of town. At the same time, town planners are pedestrianizing more areas, closing streets to cars and reducing pollution.

Rubber bounces back

The treads (gripping patterns) on tyres (tires) wear away until the tyre is too smooth to grip the road. Car owners throw away the old tyres and buy new ones. Like metal and plastic, rubber does not bio-degrade (decay naturally) easily. Tyres can be reused by being shredded and turned into tiny chips of rubber. These can be melted down to make asphalt for covering roads.

The pace of technology

New cars now have fuel-saving devices added such as stop-start technology and cruise control. Stop-start makes the engine cut out at traffic lights, and start again when the clutch is pressed, so the car spends less time idling (when the engine is running but the car isn't moving). Cruise control is when the car can be set to go at a constant low speed, which avoids speeding and uses less fuel.

Recycling cars

Most of the materials used in cars can now be recycled, and new technology means that this is now done more cheaply and efficiently so that reusable material can be produced without using too much energy in the process. This means that not so much of a scrapped car ends up in dumps or buried in landfill sites.

City smog

China produces the largest amount of greenhouse emissions than any other country in the world. Chinese people often wear masks on days when the pollution is really high. These runners are wearing them while taking part in the Beijing Marathon, 2014.

BRAKING SYSTEMS

CARS HAVE two types of brakes. Parking brakes lock the rear wheels when the car is standing still. They are controlled by the handbrake lever inside the car. Brakes for when the car is moving are usually made of steel discs fixed to each wheel. They are called disc brakes and are controlled by the brake pedal inside the car. The disc brakes attached to the car's road wheels work just like the model disc brake in the project. Putting the brakes on too sharply when a car is moving can cause a skid, when the wheels lock and the tyres (tires) slide on the road surface.

Antilock braking systems (ABS) measure the road surface conditions and stop the car going into a skid. This is done by making the disc brakes come on and off very quickly, so that the wheels don't lock. Some cars are now also fitted with automatic braking, when a car's sensors detect when a collision is about to occur and begins braking to avoid a crash.

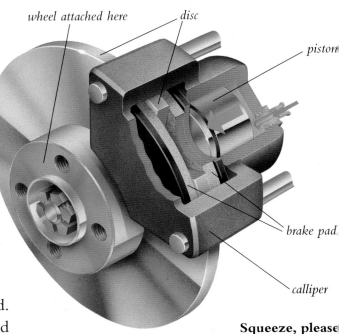

wheel attached here *disc* *piston* *brake pad* *calliper*

Squeeze, please

The disc brake unit's disc is attached to a turning hub. This is bolted to the road wheel. When the driver presses the brake pedal, fluid is squeezed down a tube to the piston on the side of the disc brake. The piston presses together two pads, one on either side of the disc, gripping it firmly and stopping it from turning. As the disc slows, so does the car wheel.

Ready, steady, go

A stock car (modified saloon car) moves off from stop very suddenly. The driver builds up the power in the engine. When the engine is near full power, the driver quickly releases the brakes. Because the wheels suddenly start spinning incredibly quickly, the tyres roar and whine against the hard ground, and burn with the heat of the friction (rubbing) against the road. The burning rubber turns into smoke which billows in white clouds around the rear wheels.

Water sports

Rally drivers have to deal with extreme conditions such as dirt tracks, mud, snow and water. Powerful brakes help them to keep control of the cars. After going through water, a rally car's brakes would be wet. This makes them less effective because there is less friction. The brake pads slip against the wet disc. The driver has to press the brake pedal with a pumping action to get rid of the water.

DISC BRAKE

You will need: *scissors, 40cm/16in length of fabric, circular cardboard box with lid, masking tape, pencil, 20cm/8in length of 12mm/¼in diameter wood dowel, glue, 7x11cm/3x5in piece of sandpaper, 6x10cm/2½x4in wood block, two plastic cups, insulation tape.*

1 Use the scissors to cut a 40cm/16in long strip from the fabric. You may have to use special fabric cutting scissors if ordinary scissors are not sharp enough.

2 Take the strip of fabric you have cut out and wrap it around the rim of the circular cardboard box. Secure it firmly in place with small pieces of masking tape.

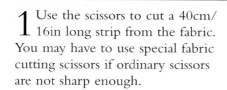

3 Make a hole in the middle of the box's lid with a pencil. Twist the pencil until it comes through the base of the box. Now gently push the wood dowel through both holes.

4 Spread lots of glue on to the sandpaper's smooth side. Wrap the sandpaper carefully over the top of the wood block, pressing to stick it.

6 Spin the lid fast on the dowel. As it spins, bring the sandpaper into contact with the edge of the lid and see how it stops the lid turning. Test your brake disc and see how quickly and how gradually you can stop the lid.

5 Stand two plastic cups upside down on a flat surface. Rest either end of the wooden dowel on each cup. Cut two small pieces of insulation tape. Use them to fix each end of the dowel firmly to the cup tops.

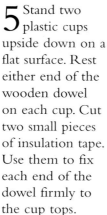

SAFETY ISSUES

RAFFIC ACCIDENTS are a constant danger. As the number of cars on the roads increased in the first half of the 1900s, the number of accidents to pedestrians and drivers increased also. During the last 50 years, ideas were put forward to reduce the scale of the problem. Gradually, most countries decided that a driver must pass a test in driving skills and governments created safety regulations for road builders and car makers to follow. In many places, drivers and passengers are now required by law to wear seat belts, and driving while under the influence of alcohol or using a handheld phone is forbidden. New cars have built-in safety features such as body parts that resist crushing, and airbags that inflate to lessen the impact of collisions. Emergency services deal more quickly with injured people. All these advances mean that in many countries there are fewer road deaths than there were 20 years ago, even though there are more cars.

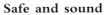

Safe and sound

If a car moving at the relatively slow speed of 30kmh/20mph stopped suddenly, a child could be thrown forwards and injured. To prevent this, the child can be strapped into a specially designed chair that is fixed securely to a car seat. It also stops the child from distracting the driver.

Bags of life

Experts who test cars for safety use crash-test dummies that react just like human bodies. These dummies are being protected by airbags, which were introduced into European production-line cars by Volvo in the 1980s. Airbags act as a kind of life-saving cushion, protecting a person from being thrown into the dashboard or the seat in front. The airbags inflate with gases as soon as sensors detect the first moment of a collision.

Not a care in the world

In the early days of motoring, people were much less aware of road safety as there were very few cars. In this 1906 drawing, a rich young man-about-town leans over the back of his car seat. He does not have to worry about where he is going because he has a chauffeur to drive him. Yet even the chauffeur is careless and narrowly avoids hitting a pedestrian in front of the car.

Pain in the neck

When a car stops suddenly, a person's head is jolted forwards and then sharply backwards. This can cause damage to the neck called whiplash. It often results in serious injury. Car manufacturers have invented seats that slide backwards and then tilt. The pictures show (1) the seat in normal position, (2) the seat sliding back, and (3) the seat's backrest tilting over. Combined with the headrest at the top, this seat design helps reduce whiplash.

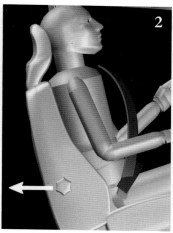
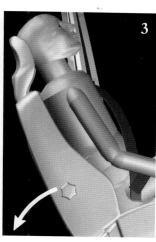

Traffic control

Before traffic control measures were introduced, accidents were common. In 1914, the first electric traffic light was installed in Cleveland, Ohio in the USA. Traffic lights control the flow of cars through road junctions.

Grand slam

When cars collide with each other at high speed their bodywork (outer metal shell) smashes and twists. Safety engineers test the strength of a car's bodywork by hitting sample cars with powerful robot sledges. Wires attached to the car detect information about safety weak points. This information is used to improve the safety of materials and designs used in cars.

Major obstruction ahead

When a large truck tips over and spills its cargo, it creates all kinds of problems. Fire crews rescue anyone who is trapped in a vehicle, and medical teams treat any injured people. The police and fire crews direct the removal of the spilt cargo. Heavy cranes are needed to shift the truck. Although drivers are diverted to other routes, traffic jams build up that can stretch for long distances.

GOOD DESIGN

Car MAKERS use large teams of people to create their new cars. Stylists, design engineers and production engineers combine with the sales team to develop a car that people will want to buy. Before the new car is announced to the public, models are made. A quarter-sized clay model is tested in a wind tunnel to investigate the car's aerodynamics (how air flows over its shape). Finally, a prototype (early version) of the car is built and tested for road handling, engine quality and comfort.

Sleek and shiny
Computer design software allows car designers to create a three-dimensional image of a new car design.

Art on wheels
An old VW Beetle has been decorated in exciting bright designs. A car's paintwork is called its livery.

MODEL CAR

You will need: two A4/8½x11in sheets of cardboard, pair of compasses (compass), ruler, scissors, glue, brush, bradawl (awl), 15cm/6in square of stiff red card (card stock), pliers, paper clips, two 10cm/4in lengths of 12mm/½in dowel, masking tape.

Wire basket
Three-dimensional, wire-frame (see-through) computer images allow designers to see how the shapes of the car fit together.

1 Draw and cut out four 2.5cm/1in and eight 6cm/2½in diameter cardboard circles. Glue the larger ones together to make four wheels. Glue a smaller circle to the middle of each.

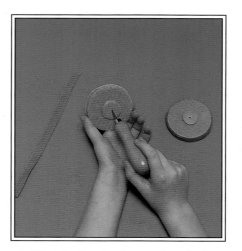

2 Use the bradawl to make a hole in the middle of each wheel. Cut four 4mm/⅛in strips of red card. Wrap one around each of the wheel rims. Glue the overlapping ends.

3 Push straightened paper clips into the holes and bend the outer ends with pliers. Fix the wheels to the two pieces of dowel by pushing the paper clips into the ends.

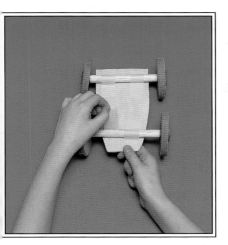

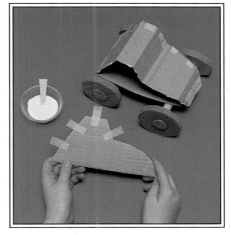

4 Cut a piece of cardboard to 8x15cm/3x6in. Trim one end to 6cm/2½in wide. Tape the two axles to the board, one at each end. Leave space for the wheels to turn freely.

5 Cut another piece of cardboard 8x35cm/3x14in. Double it over and bend into a cab shape. Tape the loose ends together. Stick the base of the cab shape to the car base.

6 Cut two more cardboard shapes 15cm/6in long and 10cm/4in high. Trim them to the same shape as the side of your car cab. Attach the sides to the cab with tape.

DECORATE YOUR CAR

You will need: *two shades of acrylic paints, medium paintbrushes, pencil, three A5/6x8½in sheets of stiff card (card stock) in different shades, a piece of white card (card stock), two felt-tip pens, scissors, glue.*

1 Remove the wheels from your car. Paint the sides and top of the cab with one of the two shades of paint. Paint two coats and leave to dry.

2 Draw exciting designs for the sides of the car, and a driver to go behind the windscreen (windshield). Fill them in with the felt-tip pens.

3 Let the paint dry for a couple of hours. Cut the designs out of the card. Glue them to the sides and back of the car. Paint the wheels with the shade of paint not yet used.

4 Replace the wheels when they are dry. Now your car looks just like a real street machine. Cut photographs of cars from magazines for ideas for new designs.

FRICTION AND OIL

When the parts of an engine move, they touch and create friction (rub against one another). The more quickly and often they move, the more friction there is. This makes the engine parts grow hot, but if they become too hot they expand and no longer fit properly. When this happens, the parts jam against one another and the engine seizes up.

Oil, a slippery liquid, lubricates the car engine. It is stored in a part of the engine, from where it is pumped on to the moving parts. Eventually the oil gets dirty with soot and dirt from outside. The dirty oil must be drained, and clean oil put in at regular intervals. Ball bearings help other moving parts of the car turn against each other. The project shows you how marbles can behave like ball bearings to reduce friction.

Oil giant
Car ownership grew steadily in the 1930s. This created a big demand for new car products. People wanted to keep their cars running smoothly and safely. Most of all, car owners needed engine oil that was always high quality, wherever and whenever they bought it. Oil companies spent a lot of money on advertisements, telling people that their particular brand of oil was the best.

Sea changes
Oil rigs drill deep into the sea-bed to find crude (natural) oil. Car lubricating oil is made from this. Pumps in the rig draw the crude oil up from the sea-bed into pipes leading to refineries on land. Impurities are removed from the crude oil in the refineries. This makes it light enough to use in car engines.

Extra Jag
High-performance sports cars, such as the Jaguar E-Type of the 1960s, need a particularly light oil. Otherwise their powerful engines will not run smoothly. The E-Type engine in this car has six cylinders (most car engines have four), which generate the power needed to accelerate to a top speed of 240kmh/150mph. Over time a thick oil would clog the oil ways, leading to friction and wear and tear of many engine parts.

Oil guzzler

Large luxury cars need a lot of oil. This 1958 Lincoln Continental has a huge 8-cylinder engine to lubricate. During the 1950s oil was very cheap and so American car makers had less reason to think about the costs of running cars as carefully as they have in more recent years.

Oil-free

Electric cars do not require oil because they have electric motors rather than an internal combustion engine, so there is no friction to be lubricated. High-spec electric cars like this Tesla Model S run on batteries, which when fully charged will last for over 480km/300 miles.

BALL BEARINGS

You will need: A4/8½x11in sheet of stiff card (card stock), scissors, masking tape, five 1x20cm/5½x8in strips of corrugated cardboard, 16 glass marbles.

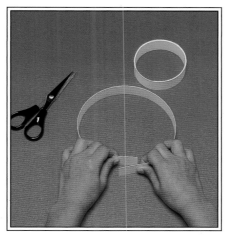

1 Cut two strips of stiff card, both 1.5cm/⅜in wide. The first one should be 20cm/8in long and the second 10cm/4in long. Make both into circles. Tape the ends together.

2 Use the strips of corrugated cardboard to line the inside of the larger card circle. Put all five strips in, and make sure that they are packed very closely together.

3 Place the smaller circle inside. Try to turn it against the corrugated cardboard. The corrugations create friction so it is not easy to turn the smaller circle.

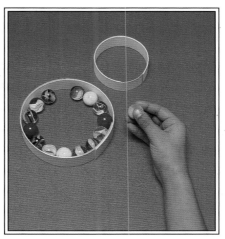

4 Take the smaller circle and the corrugated strips out of the large circle. Now line the inside of the larger circle with the marbles until there are no gaps between them.

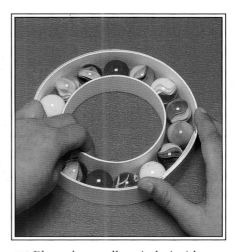

5 Place the smaller circle inside the larger one again. Turn the small circle. It moves very easily. The smooth surface of the glass marbles creates much less friction.

CLASSIC MODELS

DIFFERENT PEOPLE collect different kinds of cars. Those who are looking for style collect classic cars (at least 20 years old). Often the cars come from the 1950s, 1960s and 1970s. Owners take pride in the exceptional design and quality of the vehicles. For example, Rolls-Royces of any era look distinctive, and their engines and other mechanical parts were made with unusual care and the very best materials. High-performance classic sports cars such as the 1968 Aston Martin DB4, the 1960s Ford Mustang, the 1988 Porsche 959, the 1991 Acura NSX Coupe, and the 1995 Mitsubishi 3000GT VR4 Spyder are popular too. Collectors of classic cars often belong to specialist clubs, which them to find spare parts and to meet other people who are interested in the same models. Motor museums, such as the Museum of Automobile History in the USA, the National Motor Museum in the Britain and the Porsche Museum in Germany, exhibit classic cars.

One of the greats
Few sports cars are as eagerly collected as the 1949 Jaguar XK120. It combines high speed with good looks. Its six-cylinder engine has double overhead camshafts (to control the valves in the cylinder heads). It can reach speeds of up to 193kmh/120mph.

Bumper beauty
American car makers of the 1950s such as Cadillac created cars that shone with large areas of chrome (shiny metal). Bumpers (fenders) and radiator grilles had streamlined shapes to catch the eye.

Fly me to the Moon
The Mercedes-Benz 300SL sports car was built by hand, so only 1,400 of them were made. It has one very striking feature. Its passenger and driver doors open upwards from the roof of the car, like the famous DeLorean DMC-12 car from the *Back to the Future* movies. This design gave the car its nickname "The Gullwing", because the open doors look like a seagull. It is not very easy to get in and out of the car. Once inside, the driver and passenger sit close to the ground. The engine of the Gullwing was also set very low, to make sure that the driver could see over the top of the long bonnet (hood).

Air-cooled cool

The Porsche first appeared in 1939, as a higher-powered, streamlined, variation of the Volkswagen Beetle. Like the Beetle, the Porsche engine was air-cooled. The 911 series Porsche Carrera was first made in 1964. Then, in 1997, the firm produced its first water-cooled car, the 928.

FACT BOX

• The classic Jaguar E-type was Britain's fastest production-line car in 1961. Its top speed was 241kmh/150mph.

• The 1968 Ferrari 365GTB4 Daytona was one of the world's fastest cars, with a top speed of 281kmh/175mph.

• A 1926 Bentley 3-litre tourer was auctioned for £135,700/$204,490 in 2011.

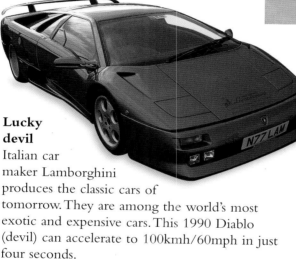

Lucky devil

Italian car maker Lamborghini produces the classic cars of tomorrow. They are among the world's most exotic and expensive cars. This 1990 Diablo (devil) can accelerate to 100kmh/60mph in just four seconds.

A country of classic cars

One way to step back in time in the world of cars is to visit Cuba. This is because for a long time Cuba had a ban on importing foreign cars, and it was also difficult to buy spare parts. The cars that Cubans drive are therefore very old but very well cared for, and it is a common sight to see a whole street full of beautiful classic cars used as Cubans' everyday vehicles.

Classic performance

The 1957 Chevy is one of the most recognizable collector cars the USA ever produced. Although it did well in its first few years, it was much later that it became so popular. With its distinctive happy-face grille and jet aircraft tail fins, it became the most sought-after used car in history.

Future classic

Bugatti is a former French high-performance car manufacturer now owned by Volkswagen. Its cars are famous for a combination of speed and beauty. The Bugatti Veyron has a top speed of 407kmh/253mph, making it the fastest production car of all time.

SPORTS CARS

SPORTS CARS, also known as roadsters, are made for speed rather than comfort. Their engines are more powerful than those in everyday cars. In addition, they usually have only two seats. That way they carry less weight than ordinary cars. A French Delage super-sports car made an international record in 1932 with a speed of 180kmh/110mph. In 2015 the Porsche 918 arrived on the scene with a top speed of 339kmh/211mph. Sports cars are driven on ordinary roads but they can also be driven in races. The Italian Lancia Delta rally car has won the World Rally Championships 46 times. The engines and bodies of sports cars are often developed from racing cars and have been tried out under demanding conditions. The Le Mans 24-hour race in France is used as a tough testing ground for sports-car engines.

Breezing along
A 1904 Mercedes was no car to drive if you caught colds easily. There was no such thing as a convertible (a sports car with a folding roof) in 1904. Even so, this Mercedes was built for speed. A restored model shows the beautiful headlamps and coachwork (bodywork) created for this masterpiece of early car engineering.

Red roadster
This is a Big Healey, one of the larger models produced by the British car maker Austin Healey. The company is also known for its small sports car, the Sprite, nicknamed Frogeye because of its bulbous headlamps. Austin Healey ceased production in 1971, but its cars are still popular with collectors.

FACT BOX
• Jaguar produced their first sports car, the SS90, in 1935.

• The Aston Martin DB5 is the car of choice of James Bond.

• The Chevrolet Camaro was first produced in 1967 and is a powerful sports car, still popular today among collectors. The 1989 model had a V-8 engine that could reach 240kmh/150mph.

• The MG sports cars are so-called because the company that made them was originally called Morris Garages.

Red bullet
The 1961 Jaguar E-Type's engine was developed from the one used in Jaguar's D-Type racing cars. Jaguar regularly took part in racing car events in the 1950s. The D-Type was a truly great racing car. It won the Le Mans 24-hour race four times between 1953 and 1957.

Pushy Porsche

The rear wing sticking out of the back of the Porsche 911 Turbo improves the flow of air over the back of the car when it travels at speed. It works by flattening out the air flow as it moves over the top of the car and down the rear. This helps to keep the car's body firmly on the road and the driver in control on tight bends.

Cool bug

The Volkswagen Beetle was always seen as a cheap family car. Then the 1968 Cabriolet appeared and surprised everyone. Volkswagen had made the engine more powerful to bring it into the same speed range as other small sports cars. It also had a flexible roof that could roll back in hot weather. This sporty Beetle is one of many changes the design has gone through since it was first produced in 1939.

Silver speeder

The Bugatti company started building high-quality sports and racing cars in 1909, first in Germany and then in France. When the firm was sold in 1956, people feared it would never make cars again. In 1991, however, the Bugatti EB110 appeared, hoping to keep the glory of the past alive. Its design, 12-valve engine and four-wheel drive were praised widely. In 1994, Bugatti closed again, but the company was later bought by Volkswagen.

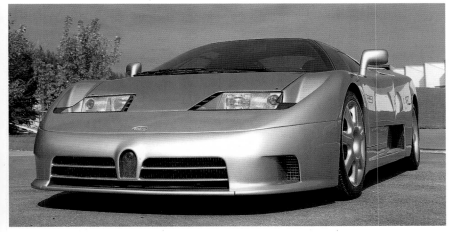

Classy convertible

The BMW (*Bayerische Motoren Werke*) company has made cars and motorcycles in Munich since 1928. In the 1970s, they began to sell more of their cars outside Germany. By the 1980s, BMWs were popular throughout the world. Although this 650i convertible from 2011 has four seats, its quick acceleration and high speed means it is still seen as a two-door sports car.

FUEL CONTROL

THE CONTROLLED flow of fuel into a car's engine is very important because it affects how the car performs. If there is too much fuel and not enough air, the engine will flood with petrol (gasoline) and won't start. If there is not enough fuel, the engine will run in a jerky way. The mixing of fuel and air occurs inside the carburettor. A piston goes down as a rod, called a camshaft, opens a valve to let the fuel and air mixture in. The valve closes and the piston goes up, compressing (squeezing) the fuel and air mixture. The spark plug fires to ignite the fuel mixture, pushing the piston down again. The piston rises again and the exhaust valve opens to release the waste gases.

The project shows you how to make a model that works in the same way as a camshaft. It opens one valve and then, as it closes the first valve, a second valve opens.

filtered air

petrol (gasoline)

fuel and air mixture

Mixing it

In cold weather, engines need more fuel to get started. In old cars the driver would pull out a choke. This caused the carburettor to increase the amount of fuel in the fuel and air mixture. All modern cars have automatic chokes now. Internal computers work out the exact mixture of fuel and air that will suit the weather conditions.

Diesel or petrol?

Like petrol, diesel is made from refined crude oil. Cars that run on diesel have slightly different engines, so you can only use one type of fuel in your car.

In search of power

Very powerful cars, such as the Lamborghini Diablo, built by the Italian car makers between 1999 and 2001, need to generate a lot of energy to accelerate (increase speed) quickly. They have 12 cylinders in their engines, burning much more fuel than an ordinary four-cylinder car. The burnt fuel creates a large amount of exhaust gas. The Diablo has four exhaust pipes at the rear of the car. Most ordinary cars have only one exhaust pipe.

AC 868 DV

ROCK AND ROLL CAMSHAFT

You will need: *scissors, 6cm/2½in square stiff card (card stock), masking tape, cardboard tube with plastic lid, pencil.*

1 Cut a 1x6cm/½x2½in strip from the card. Double it over in the middle. Hold it with your fingertips. Bend the two ends of the card away from one another.

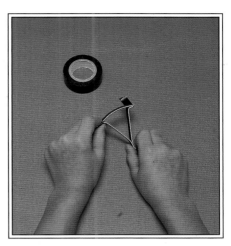

2 Cut a 1x4cm/½x1½in strip from the original piece of card. Use masking tape to fix the card strip to the bent bottom ends of the first piece. This makes a triangle shape.

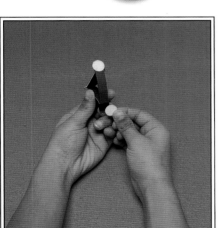

3 Use the scissors to cut out two small circle shapes from the original piece of card. Use masking tape to secure them to the bottom piece of the triangle you have made.

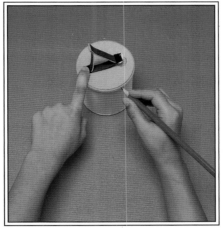

4 Put the triangle on top of the cardboard tube. The circles should touch the plastic lid. With a pencil, mark where the circles sit on the lid.

5 Using the scissors, carefully cut around the pencil marks you have made in the plastic lid of the tube. These form an inlet and an outlet.

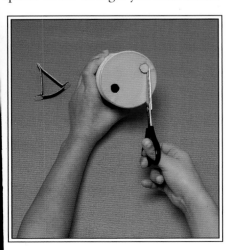

6 Now you can rock the triangle back and forth to cover and uncover the two holes one after another. This is just how a camshaft opens and shuts the inlet and outlet valves in a car's cylinder.

SUSPENSION

THE EARLIEST cars used coach wheels made of wood and metal. They gave a very bumpy ride. In the early 1900s, the French company Michelin made a rubber tyre (tire) with an inflatable inner tube. The idea came from the tyre that John Dunlop developed in the late 1800s for bicycles. The outer part of the tyre was made of rubber. Inside it had a tube filled with air. The air cushioned the car's contact with the road and driving became much more comfortable.

All car tyres had inner tubes until the 1950s. From then on, more tubeless tyres were made. In these, air is held in a web of wire and an inner tyre that fits tightly on the wheel rim. Cars use suspension systems, as well as air-filled tyres, as cushioning. Suspension systems are attached to a car's wheels to absorb impacts from the road. In modern cars, these are usually either coiled springs, shaped rubber cones or gas-filled cylinders.

Thick and thin

The engines on hot rods (cars with boosted engines) drive the rear wheels. These wheels often have thick tyres. This means there is a lot of contact between the road surface and the tyre surface, helping the car to grip the road when accelerating.

Suspension

A car's suspension system makes driving comfortable. It prevents the car from being bumped up and down too much on bumpy roads. In the early 1900s, car suspension was the same as the suspension in horse-drawn carriages. Modern cars use much more sophisticated systems. The Jaguar XKR Coupe shown here has a coiled spring system.

The suspension system is attached to each wheel. If the car goes over a 5cm/2in bump, the wheel will go up 5cm/2in too, but the car's body will move up less distance. The suspension system absorbs the impact. After going over the bump, the car's body will sink down slowly, too. Hydraulic cylinders (cylinders full of a liquid, such as oil, or gas) do this. The cylinders are called dampers, because they damp down the effect of the bump.

Taking off

Rally cars travel so quickly that when they come over the top of a hill they can leave the ground for a second or two. Then they come back down to earth with a stomach-churning bump. A hard landing can shatter a car's axles and put the car out of the competition. Rally cars take this kind of punishment hour after hour, day after day. They have to be fitted with extra-tough suspension systems.

Early tyres

This 1903 Mercedes-Benz sports car is fitted with tyres which have a rubber outer casing. Inside these were rubber tubes filled with air, just like the inner tubes in bicycle tyres. Tyre manufacturers stopped including inner tubes in car tyres from the 1950s onwards, as drivers were having too many punctures.

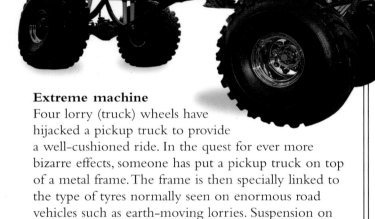

Extreme machine

Four lorry (truck) wheels have hijacked a pickup truck to provide a well-cushioned ride. In the quest for ever more bizarre effects, someone has put a pickup truck on top of a metal frame. The frame is then specially linked to the type of tyres normally seen on enormous road vehicles such as earth-moving lorries. Suspension on this scale allows the truck to travel over extremely uneven surfaces, such as a stony quarry floor.

Big smoothie

Limousines look spectacular and provide exceptional levels of comfort. Stretch limousines are the most luxurious of all. They are often used for weddings and other important events. Very long cars like this, which have been adapted to hold several people, need very good suspension. The smooth ride in a limousine is provided by extra wide tyres, and a computer-controlled suspension system that uses compressed air.

HOME FROM HOME

THE GREAT advantage of setting off on an adventure by car is that you can go where you want, when you want. It is even possible to travel to places where there may be no towns or people. Once you're there, however, what do you do when you want to go to sleep at night? One solution is to drive a special car such as a multi-purpose vehicle (MPV) or a recreational vehicle (RV). They are built to provide sleeping space. Smaller ones have car seats that will lie flat to make a bed. Larger RVs have cabins with built-in bunks, kitchens and sitting areas. They may also have televisions, music systems, microwave ovens and all the high-tech equipment that can be found in a conventional house. The interiors of top-of-the-range RVs can be built according to the buyer's preferences.

Long way from home
Long-distance truck drivers, who drive thousands of kilometres every year, often travel through regions where there are very few towns or villages. At night the driver finds a safe place to park, then sleeps in a built-in bunk on a shelf behind the driver's seat.

Open-air life
Caravans (campers) are mobile living units that can be towed from place to place by cars. Towing a caravan requires a lot of extra power from the car, so larger vehicles, like this four-wheel drive are the most suitable. A low caravan has less wind resistence when being towed.

Time travel
VW camper vans, made by the German car manufacturer Volkswagen, have been very popular for over 65 years. The owners of vintage VW camper vans are a dedicated to their vehicles, lavishing care, attention and money on their beloved wheels. These little RVs are very different from the huge luxury models that are usually sold or hired out today.

SCENTED CAR FRESHENER

You will need: *200ml/scant 1 cup water, mixing bowl, 200g/1⅔ cups plain (all-purpose) flour, wooden spoon, pie pan, pencil, bottle of essential oil, paintbrush, four shades of acrylic paint, 45cm/18in length of string.*

1 Pour the water into a mixing bowl. Stir in the flour slowly with a wooden spoon. Continue to stir until the paste thickens into a dough mixture that you can shape.

2 Place the dough mixture in the pie pan. Form the dough into a bell shape that bulges out at the bottom. Roughly shape a roof at the top and wheels underneath.

3 Wet the rough shape so it is easy to form a design on it. Smooth your fingers over the top area to make a windscreen (windshield). Shape the wheels more accurately.

4 Make small holes in the car and one larger hole in the top. Sprinkle essential oil in the holes. Bake in an oven for 45 minutes at 150°C/300°F/Gas 2.

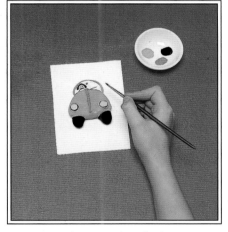

5 Once the car is cool, place it on a sheet of paper. Paint the bonnet (hood), then the details, such as a driver's face. Add lines around the headlights.

6 Leave the paint to dry. Thread the piece of string through the hole in the top of the car's windscreen. Double the string back and knot it to make a noose.

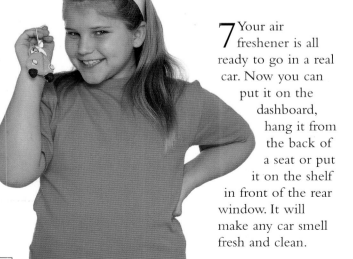

7 Your air freshener is all ready to go in a real car. Now you can put it on the dashboard, hang it from the back of a seat or put it on the shelf in front of the rear window. It will make any car smell fresh and clean.

DIFFERENT TYPES OF FUEL

WHEN CARS were first invented, and for many years afterwards, they all ran on petrol (gasoline). Because cars were very heavy, they needed a lot of petrol to make them move. Later, sports cars or racing cars used lots of fuel to reach high speeds. Today, cars of any engine size are designed to use as little fuel as possible because oil, which petrol is made from, is so expensive. Oil is also a non-renewable fuel. This means that one day it will run out. New laws have made manufacturers produce cars that use less fuel and have reduced carbon emissions. There has been a lot of research to find alternative fuels for cars. These include biofuels (fuel made from organic or vegetable matter), solar powered cars, and hybrid or electric cars, which run on batteries.

Roaring oldie
Super Street hot rodders often take the bodies of old cars and combine them with modern parts. The 1950s car body here has been joined to big tyres (tires) by a complicated suspension system. Some hot rodders use special chemical fuels such as ethanol and nitromethane. When they burn, they get much hotter than petrol. The extra heat helps them to accelerate to very high speeds.

FACT BOX
• Rising oil prices in the 1970s led to the creation of gasohol, a mixture of gasoline and ethanol, a form of alcohol. Ethanol can be made from plants such as potatoes.

• Petrol used to contain lead, which is harmful to health. Traces of lead in car exhaust fumes accumulated in children's bodies and could cause brain damage. In 1988 unleaded petrol became available and it is now compulsory (required by law).

The need for speed
Members of the Ferarri pitstop crew swarm over Michael Schumacher's car at the Spanish Grand Priz, 2002. In the middle, team members hold the hose that forces fuel into the car's tank at high pressure. Up to 100 litres/25 gallons can be pumped in in about 10 seconds. The crew's speed is essential. Every second in the pit lane equals about 60 metres/65 yards lost on the track.

Two-carb Caddy

The Cadillacs of the 1950s are reminders of a time when petrol was cheap and people could afford to run big, heavy cars. In the 1970s, the price of oil rose dramatically, so petrol became much more expensive. This 1955 Cadillac Fleetwood had two carburettors, even though most cars built at that time would have had just one. The second carburettor was needed because the Fleetwood used so much petrol.

Hand-built hybrid

The most fuel efficient car invented so far is thought to be the Volkswagen XL1. So far only 250 have been made, as they have to be constructed by hand, and they cost £92,490/$138,156 each. The car is a hybrid, which means it runs on electricity and diesel. It can travel for 503km/313 miles on 4.5 litres/1 gallon of fuel. The car is made from very lightweight materials, replacing some of the steel parts with carbon fibre, and is very streamlined. It also has 'scissor' doors, which open upwards from a hinge at the front of the door, looking rather like the wings of a beetle.

Biofuel

Diesel cars can be converted to run with biofuels, such as sunflower or corn oil. The cars can even run on waste vegetable oil from restaurants after it has been used to cook with. Some people are worried that this isn't as environmentally safe as was first believed, however, and feel that more research needs to be done.

Running on sunshine

Some electrical cars are already indirectly running on solar power by using electricity that has been generated by solar panels. Scientists are trying to invent a car that can run directly on power from the sun, which basically means a solar panel on wheels. Some interesting experiments have been done, including these cars from Nuon Solar Team, competing in the 2015 Bridgestone World Solar Challenge. The Ford C-Max Solar Energi Concept car is also being developed, which looks more like an ordinary car.

SPEED RECORDS

In more than a hundred years of car building, cars have reached faster and faster speeds. In 1899, the Belgian inventor Camille Jenatzy was the first person to drive a car faster than 100kmh/62mph. The car, designed by Jenatzy himself, ran on electricity. In the same year, Sir Charles Wakefield created his Castrol Motor Oil company. The company awards the official trophy for the land-speed record to drivers who break the record. The trophy was first won in 1914 by the Englishman L.G. Hornsted. He reached a speed of 200kmh/124mph in a car from the German car maker Benz. Since then 38 other people have broken the record. The last person to succeed was the British RAF Tornado pilot Andy Green, on 13 October 1997. His car, powered by two jet engines, broke the sound barrier (sound travels at a speed of 1,226kmh/762mph), reaching 1,228kmh/763mph.

Satisfaction at last
Between December 1898 and April 1899, there were no less than six attempts to beat the land-speed record. All of them were made by drivers in electric cars. The fastest, in April, was the Belgian Camille Jenatzy who reached 106kmh/66mph. He called his car *La Jamais Contente* (Never Satisfied) because he had already tried to set the land-speed record twice before.

Gas-powered wheels
Finding a long, flat, hard surface to travel on is very important when trying to set a speed record on land. Donald Campbell thundered across the Lake Eyre Salt Flats in Australia in 1964. He reached a speed of 649kmh/403mph in his gas-turbine powered car Bluebird. He was following in the footsteps of his father Malcolm, who had set nine land-speed records.

Golden goer
The Golden Arrow set a land-speed record of 370kmh/230mph on 11 March 1929. The enormous, streamlined car was powered by a Napier-Lion aircraft engine. It flashed along the hard, white sand at Daytona Beach in Florida, USA. The driver was Major Henry Seagrave. After setting the land-speed record, Seagrave went on to set the world water-speed record.

Expensive record

The Black Rock Desert in Nevada, USA was the scene for another record-breaking attempt in 1983. On this dried lake bed, in blistering desert heat, Richard Noble set a new record of 1,018kmh/633mph. He was driving the specially made jet-engine powered Thrust 2. Making a speed record attempt costs a lot of money. The advertisements plastered all over the car are for businesses that donated money for this record attempt.

Supersonic car

In 1997 Andy Green drove the Thrust SSC at an incredible 1,228kmh/763mph. He did not just set a new world land-speed record, he went faster than the speed of sound (1,226kmh/762mph). Until then, speeds greater than that of sound had only been possible in flight. Andy was used to the speed because he was a jet pilot for the British Royal Air Force.

The next generation

The British-built Bloodhound SSC is set to become the next car to break the record, with a speed of 1,600kmh/1,000mph, but it is still being developed. Andy Green, who has held the land speed record since 1997, is also the driver of the Bloodhound. The car, which looks like a space rocket, was unveiled to the public in London in 2015.

MOTORWAYS AND FREEWAYS

Before the 1800s, most roads were just earth tracks. Some roads in cities and towns were made of stone and wood blocks, which gave a rough ride. Macadam roads (roads covered in a hard layer of tiny stones) were a great improvement in the 1800s, but with the invention of cars at the end of the 1800s, new road surfaces were needed. Roads made of asphalt (a mixture of bitumen and stone) and concrete offered the hardness and smoothness that cars needed to travel safely and quickly.

The first motorway (freeway) was completed in 1932 in Germany, between Cologne and Bonn. As car ownership grew during the second half of the 1900s, road building programmes followed. Some people think there are too many roads and protest against building more because they want to protect the countryside.

Multi-lane moves

Car ownership and use has grown relentlessly, and freeways in the USA have grown, too. In the last 30 years the freeways have increased in size from four lanes to 12 lanes, and even to 16 lanes on some stretches.

Pay as you go

The enormous costs of building motorways can be partly paid for by charging a toll (payment for using a road). The road owners set up barriers through which a car must pass to drive on to the road. Drivers crossing this toll plaza near New York City, stop at booths to buy tickets that allow them to continue on the freeway.

Keep calm

Traffic calming is the name given to the different ways of slowing down traffic speed. Building speed bumps or humps in the road is one example of traffic calming. The speed bumps force drivers to slow down in areas where there is a lot of housing. Slower car speeds help to prevent accidents.

Going places

Modern countries need well-built roads so that goods and people can travel easily between cities and towns. This is Interstate 35 approaching the American city of Minneapolis. It is part of the vast interstate highway system that links the entire country.

Major to minor

Road networks are much easier to understand from the air. A looped road (cloverleaf) links two major highways. Long curving roads such as these allow drivers to switch between major roads without having to stop at a junction. The roads that link up major roads are called slip or access roads.

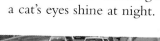

Night guide

Small glass reflectors called catseyes help drivers to see the road at night. The catseyes are set at regular intervals in the middle of the road. They gleam brightly when a car's headlights shine on them. The British inventor Percy Shaw cam up with the idea in 1933, after noticing how a cat's eyes shine at night.

The long and winding road

There are still many narrow old roads in remote areas, which twist and turn for kilometres through beautiful countryside. There is much less traffic on country roads, and they offer an enjoyable test of driving skills. Four-wheel drive vehicles handle particularly well on the tight corners and steep slopes.

Roadworks ahead

Modern roads carry a lot of traffic and need constant repair and maintenance. They cannot simply be shut down while that happens. Instead, some lanes are closed for repair while others remain open. The long lines of plastic cones on this stretch of road prevent traffic from using one of the lanes to protect workers further ahead.

BADGES AND MASCOTS

CAR MANUFACTURERS take pride in the work that goes into the machines that they make. They put badges, logos or symbols on their cars to show which company made the car. The badges are usually found on the car bonnet (hood), where they are easy to spot. There are many car makers all over the world, and they each make a different badge. The instantly recognizable designs of the most prestigious companies, such as the silver lady on Rolls-Royces or the three-spoked circle on Mercedes cars, suggest elegance or power. Other celebrated symbols are the rearing horse on the front of cars made by the Italian Ferrari company, and the VW symbol used on Volkswagen cars. Sometimes these badges are called mascots, perhaps because car makers see them as a symbol of good luck. In this project, you can make your own car mascot to symbolize the kind of car you like.

Leading lady
All Rolls-Royce cars carry a winged figure mascot on the bonnet. It is called The Spirit of Ecstasy and was created by the sculptor Charles Sykes. The figure first appeared on Rolls-Royce cars in 1911. In modern Rolls-Royces, the mascot folds down backwards into the bonnet in an accident to avoid injury.

MAGIC MASCOT

You will need: A4/8½x11in sheet of cardboard, pencil, scissors, masking tape, bradawl (awl), glue, matchstick, newspaper, fork, 250g/2¼ cups flour, 200ml/scant 1 cup water, silver spray paint, fine paintbrush, black paint.

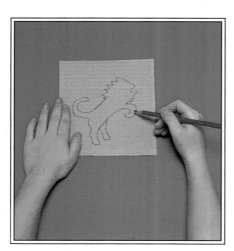

1 Cut a piece measuring 20x15cm/8x6in from the cardboard. Use a pencil to draw the outline of the shape you want to put on your car on the cardboard.

2 Use the scissors to cut roughly around the mascot shape. Then cut around the outline accurately. Be careful not to cut off any of the detail in your drawing.

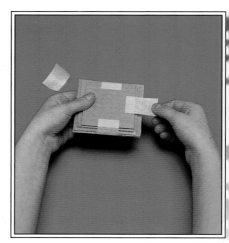

3 Cut three square pieces from the cardboard, one 5cm/2in, one 6cm/2½in and one 7cm/3in. Tape the smallest on top of the medium one and those on top of the largest.

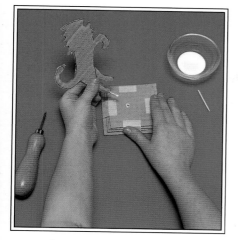

4 Make a hole in the middle of the base with the bradawl. Put a glued matchstick in the bottom of your mascot. Insert it into the hole in the base so that it stands upright.

5 Tear strips of newspaper. Mix flour and water with a fork, to make a thick paste. Dip the paper in the mixture. Apply the wet paper to the mascot in three layers.

6 When the newspaper is dry, spray your mascot with spray paint. Be careful to point the can downwards, away from you. Put a piece of paper under the badge.

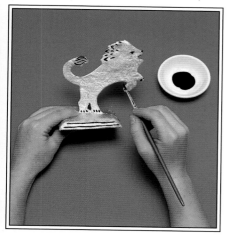

7 Use the paintbrush to apply black lines on the mascot where you want to show more detail. For example this one shows detail of the lion's mane, tail and paws.

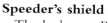

Speeder's shield
The badge on Porsche cars is like a medieval coat of arms. In the past, important people made decorations on shield shapes to tell others who their ancestors were and where they came from.

8 Your finished mascot could form the start of a great collection. You could copy other car mascots that you like. There are many more to choose from.

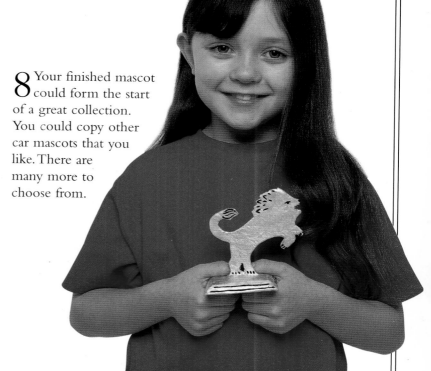

Roar of power
Jaguar cars used the model of the leaping jaguar as their mascot for many years. More recent models do not have the statuette on the bonnet. They have been declared illegal because they could cause injury to pedestrians in an accident.

THE FUTURE

THE CARS of the future already exist, but only as the still-secret designs of car makers. Embedded computers have allowed the biggest changes in cars in the last 20 years. They can now control intelligent keys, engine performance control, satellite navigation aids, start-stop technology, memorized seat settings and cruise control systems. They can also help the driver with parking and put windscreen (windshield) wipers and headlights on automatically. Some people worry that computers now have too much control over our cars. Designers and engineers are still improving fuel-efficient cars, and it is predicted that by 2040 half of all new cars will be hybrids. Self-driving cars are very close to becoming a reality. So are cars that communicate with each other using wireless signals to send information about their speed and direction. Of all the many developments that will occur, one is almost certain. There will be even more cars on the roads.

Hot item
Cars powered by energy from the sun (solar power) would be better for the environment than petrol (gasoline) engine cars. Photo-electric cells on the back of the car turn energy from the sun's rays into electricity. This energy is stored in batteries inside the car. The batteries then supply power to the engine. At the moment this method can only store enough energy to power small cars. Scientists are trying to find a way to use solar power in bigger vehicles.

Smart motorways
Intelligent motorways (freeways) are now a normal part of the road network. They use overhead signs and CCTV cameras to control the traffic flow and change speed limits through digital display boards. This helps to reduce or control congestion. The technology first developed from using electronic screens to warn drivers of hazards ahead. Sometimes there are too many instructions to drivers in a short amount of time, and so now cars are being developed that can respond automatically to these warnings.

Neat package

Car makers first produced microcars such as the BMW Isetta in the 1950s and 1960s. In 1994 the Smart car, owned and produced by Daimler AG, was introduced. Extra-small vehicles such as these are ideal for short journeys in built-up areas and are much easier to park. They are also very economical to run. The Smart car is so short (2.5m/8ft) that it can park in half a space, at right angles to the pavement (sidewalk).

Three-wheel dream

One-person cars seem an obvious answer to many traffic problems. They are not always a hit with drivers, however. The British inventor Sir Clive Sinclair produced the electric-powered Sinclair C5 in 1985. The vehicle was not very popular, and was soon taken out of production.

Self-driving car

This car can drive by itself. Just a few years ago it was thought that the technology to make this happen was a long way in the future, but now Google has made a car that can continue at a set speed and planned route all by itself, a bit like the autopilot on a plane. The cars are still being developed but by 2020 it will probably be possible to buy an autonomous car.

A car that cares

This is a concept car still in development but it includes several technological advances that will probably be part of many new cars soon. Its features include autonomous driving, iris recognition (whereby the car starts by identifying your eye), traffic forecasting and remotely controlled home appliances. The car can also detect and measure biological life signs, and can give a warning if it finds any problems with its driver's heartbeat, blood pressure or body temperature.

GLOSSARY

accelerator pedal
The pedal beneath the driver's foot that controls the flow of fuel to a car engine.

air cooled
An engine in which the heat is carried away, not by water, but by air.

air pollution
The reduction of the oxygen content in the air we breath with poisonous gases such as carbon monoxide.

airbag
A cushion stored in front of car seats that automatically inflates in a crash, protecting the driver and passengers.

amphibious car
A car that travels on land and in water.

antilock braking systems (ABS)
A specially designed braking system that avoids wheels locking and skidding when the brakes are applied.

asphalt
A mixture of bitumen and concrete used to give roads a hard, smooth, weatherproof surface.

ball bearing
A hardened steel ball, often arranged with other ball bearings around a turning surface to ease movement.

battery
A container of chemicals holding a charge of electricity.

brake
A pad or disc that slows a moving surface down by pressing it.

bubble car
The name given in the 1950s and 1960s to microcars such as the BMW Isetta, because of their round shape.

bumper
The protective, wraparound metal or rubber barrier that protects the front and rear of a car.

cabriolet
A car with a flexible roof that can be folded away into the rear of the car.

camshaft
A shaft or rod that is driven and timed with the engine crankshaft. Lobes rotate on the camshaft, opening and closing the inlet and exhaust valves in the cylinder head.

carbon monoxide
A poisonous gas that is a by-product of burning petrol.

carburettor
A unit that controls the fuel mixture entering the combustion chamber.

chequered flag
A black-and-white square patterned flag that a race controller waves as a car crosses the finishing line in a race.

chrome
A reflective metal used to cover car fittings such as bumpers and radiator grilles to make them look shiny.

classic car
A car that, because of special qualities of design and workmanship, is collected and restored.

coachwork
The outside body of a car.

convertible
A car that can be driven with or without a roof.

crankshaft
The part that transmits the four-stroke movement of the pistons to the car's driveline and road wheels.

custom car
A car that that is adapted by its owner to make it look or drive differently.

cylinder
A hollow tube in which a piston moves.

dashboard
The vertical surface that contains the instruments facing a driver inside a car.

drag racer
A car specially designed to take part in short, high-speed acceleration races.

flatbed
A small truck with a driver's cabin at the front and an open, horizontal platform at the rear.

Formula One
The class of racing car that has the most powerful engine specification.

four-wheel drive
A car in which power from the engine can be transferred to all four wheels, not just to the front or rear wheels.

friction
The rubbing of one surface against another surface.

fuel
A substance, such as petrol, that is burned to provide energy.

fuel efficient
Designed to use as little fuel as possible while ensuring normal speed and power.

gas
A non-solid, non-liquid substance given off when petrol burns. Also the name often used in the USA for petrol.

gears
Toothed wheels designed to interact with each other to transfer motion.

hot rod
A car in which the engine has been specially treated to allow it to accelerate rapidly and travel at high speed.

hydraulic
Worked by the pressure of fluid carried in pipes.

inner tube
A rubber tube filled with air contained inside the tyres of older vehicles.

internal combustion
The burning of fuel in a closed chamber to generate power.

limousine
Luxurious closed-bodied car, featuring a glass partition behind the driver.

lubrication
The smoothing of friction between the parts of an engine, usually with oil.

microcar
A particularly small car, designed to minimize traffic congestion in cities.

motorway
Mulit-lane road allowing traffic to travel long distances at speed.

mudguard
The wide wing of metal around a car wheel that prevents mud and stones from flying up off the road.

off-road vehicle (ORV)
A car that can drive on surfaces other than smooth, tarmac roads. Also known as sport utility vehicles (SUVs).

oil
A thick, black liquid found under the surface of the Earth from which petrol and other products can be made.

oxygen
The gas in the Earth's atmosphere that living creatures with lungs breathe.

pedestrian
A person who travels on foot.

petrol
The easily burned liquid made from oil that is the main fuel for internal combustion engines. Commonly known as gasoline in the USA.

pickup
A small truck with a cab at the front and a flat platform over the rear wheels.

production line
A way of building machines in which all the parts are added one by one in a continuous process in a factory.

prototype
The first attempt to build a working model of a machine from the design.

radiator
A container of water from which water is pumped around the engine to prevent overheating.

recreational vehicle (RV)
A car designed for being driven on roads other than tarmac, but not for very extreme surfaces such as fine sand, shallow riverbeds or rocks.

robot
A machine that is built to perform particular tasks automatically.

rubber
A liquid taken from rubber trees that, when treated, forms a thick, flexible material suitable for making tyres.

seat belt
A safety strap worn by drivers and passengers to prevent injury in the case of an accident.

speedometer
The dial on a car's dashboard that displays the speed at which the vehicle is moving.

sports car
An open or closed car built for performance, usually with two seats.

sport utility vehicles (SUVs)
Cars that are built for driving on rough surfaces such as roads without tarmac.

steam engine
An engine powered by the steam (water vapour) created by heating water.

steering mechanism
The combined system of steering wheel, rack and pinion mechanism and wheels that allows a driver to steer a car.

stock car
An ordinary car that has been adapted to make it suitable for racing. Also known as a rally car.

streamlining
Shaping a car's body so that it can travel with low air resistance.

suspension system
The springs and other shock absorbers that cushion the movement of a car's wheels on the road.

veteran car
Any car built before 1905.

vintage car
Any car built between 1919 and 1930.

wind tunnel
A large chamber in which powerful draughts of air are blown over a car to test and measure how much air resistance the car shows.

INDEX

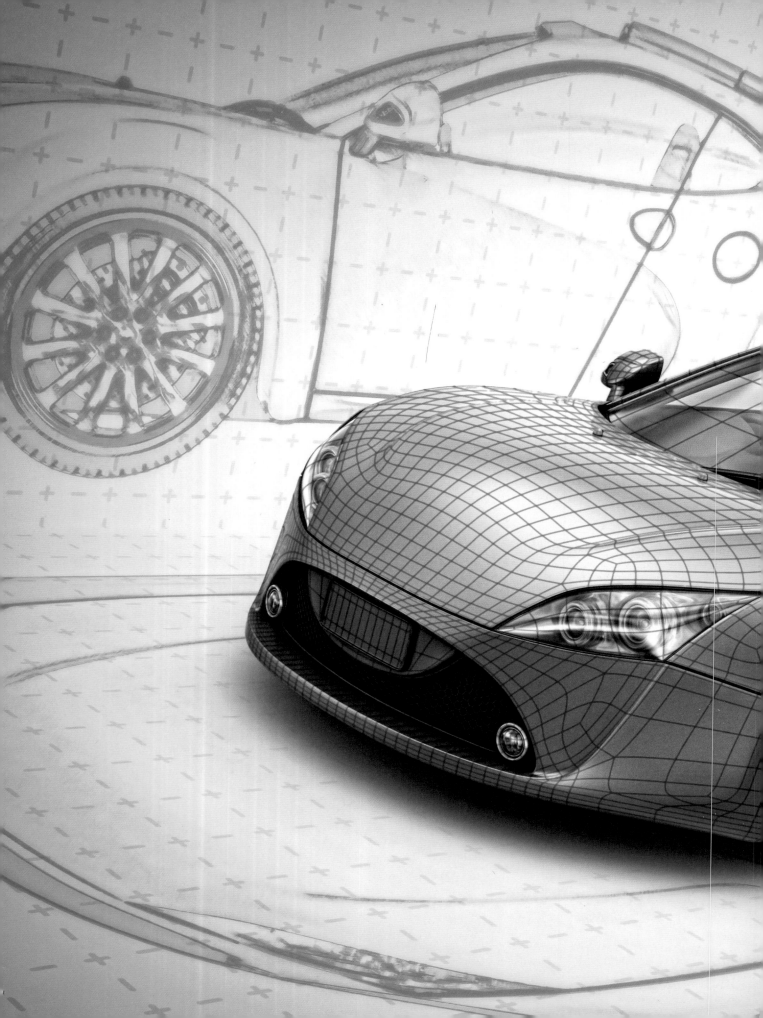